Queen
and
Consort

Elizabeth and Philip

60 Years of Marriage

Coronation photographic portrait of the Queen and her Consort, the Duke of Edinburgh.

Queen and Consort

Elizabeth and Philip

60 Years of Marriage

Lynne Bell, Arthur Bousfield & Garry Toffoli

THE DUNDURN GROUP
TORONTO

Designer: Erin Mallory
Copyeditor: Jennifer Gallant
Printer: Transcontinental

Bell, Lynne (L. Lynne)
    Queen and consort : Elizabeth and Philip : 60 years of marriage / Lynne Bell, Arthur Bousfield, Garry Toffoli.

ISBN 978-1-55002-725-9

    1. Elizabeth II, Queen of Great Britain, 1926- --Marriage. 2. Philip, Prince, consort of Elizabeth II, Queen of Great Britain, 1921-. 3. Marriages of royalty and nobility--Great Britain--History--20th century. 4. Princes--Great Britain--Biography. 5. Queens--Great Britain--Biography. I. Bousfield, Arthur, 1943- II. Toffoli, Garry, 1953- III. Title.

DA590.B42 2007   941.085092'2   C2007-904673-8

1   2   3   4   5   11   10   09   08   07

Illustration Credits

Many of the historical, copyright-expired illustrations and some contemporary illustrations are from the collection of The Canadian Royal Heritage Trust. The credits for other illustrations are as follows:

Art Gallery of Hamilton: 53 (bottom)
Arthur Edwards, MBE: 90, 91, 92
AP: 127, 143 (bottom), 165
B. Nowak: 137
Camera Press Ltd: 86
CP: 93, 95, 116, 119 (left), 173
Duke of Edinburgh's Award: 150 (right)
Garry Toffoli: 78, 124 (top right and bottom right), 131
Government of the Northwest Territories: 151
Jayne Fincher: 68 (bottom)
Janet Huse: 33, 97, 175, 176 (left)
Jaroslav Huta: 75
Josef Brousek: 124 (bottom left)
Karsh: 118
Lisa Mitchell: 103 (top and bottom), 110 (right), 114 (bottom), 119 (right), 124 (top left), 132, 144 (right), 174
London Picture Service: 68 (left), 69 (right), 176
Lynne Bell: 100 (left and right), 105, 114 (top), 121, 158, 160 (bottom)
Monarchy Canada: 87, 112, 133
Natalie Bullen: 113 (bottom)
National Archives: 149 (top right)
Norman Parkinson: 66, 117 (right)
PA: 138, 176 (right)
Prescott-Pickup & Co. Ltd: 172
Reuters: 156
Royal Canadian Mint: 160 (top)
South African Digest: 67 (right)
Stacey Connolly & Rand MacKay, Dept of Veterans' Affairs: 140, 142
UPI: 128
Victor Pilon, Dept of Canadian Heritage: 112

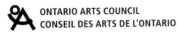

Conseil des Arts du Canada   Canada Council for the Arts

Canada

ONTARIO ARTS COUNCIL
CONSEIL DES ARTS DE L'ONTARIO

We acknowledge the support of the **Canada Council for the Arts** and the **Ontario Arts Council** for our publishing program. We also acknowledge the financial support of the **Government of Canada** through the **Book Publishing Industry Development Program** and **The Association for the Export of Canadian Books**, and the **Government of Ontario** through the **Ontario Book Publishers Tax Credit program** and the **Ontario Media Development Corporation**.

Care has been taken to trace the ownership of copyright material used in this book. The author and the publisher welcome any information enabling them to rectify any references or credits in subsequent editions.

J. Kirk Howard,
President

Printed and bound in Canada
www.dundurn.com

Dundurn Press
3 Church Street, Suite 500
Toronto, Ontario, Canada
M5E 1M2

Gazelle Book Services Limited
White Cross Mills
High Town, Lancaster, England
LA1 4XS

Dundurn Press
2250 Military Road
Tonawanda, NY
U.S.A. 14150

Table of Contents

Acknowledgements   10

Chapter 1   11
Wedding at Westminster

Chapter 2   27
Paths to the Abbey

Chapter 3   43
Bittersweet Pageant of Royal Weddings

Chapter 4   71
Consorts

Chapter 5   89
Queen, Prince, and People

Chapter 6   107
Managing the Family Firm

123   Chapter 7
States, Travel, and Technology

139   Chapter 8
Riding the Contentious Kingdom

163   Chapter 9
Modern Age, Modern Marriage

179   Bibliography

181   Index

The family photograph for the wedding.

Acknowledgements

The authors wish to acknowledge the gracious assistance of Countess Mountbatten of Burma in kindly answering questions by Lynne Bell and clarifying other points for *Queen and Consort*, which she did in person in Calgary and by telephone from the United Kingdom. In writing the book the authors owe a great debt of gratitude to Kirk Howard, Chairman, and the other Trustees of the Canadian Royal Heritage Trust / Fonds du patrimoine royal du Canada for allowing them access to the Trust's important collection of books, pictures, newspapers, scrapbooks, and manuscripts in both the King Louis XIV Canadian Royal Heritage Archives (particularly its Arnold McNaughten, M. Ida New and Ron Welker sub-collections) and the King George III Canadian Royal Heritage Library (Claudia Willetts Branch), and for permitting them to reproduce many items from it. They would like to thank Trust staff members Barbara Kemp, Jane Wachna, and Kent Jackson for their assistance in this regard. Arthur Edwards, MBE, was kind enough to provide pictures from H.M. The Queen's recent visit to the United States, and Gordon Schmidt generously gave permission for use of the painting by Guy LaLiberté of the Queen opening Parliament in 1957 that is on loan to the Canadian Royal Heritage Museum, Neustadt, Ontario. Among others who deserve special thanks are Karen Wood and fellow staff members of the Golden Griddle at 3080 Yonge Street, Toronto, for the tolerance, consideration, and care they showed to the authors in the throes of research, writing, and editing.

1 Wedding at Westminster

"A flash of colour on the hard road"
— *Sir Winston Churchill*

By the time the Second World War came to an end — with the surrender of Japan to the Allies on August 14, 1945 — Britain had been at war for just under six years. While the entire British Commonwealth and Empire and its allies rejoiced at the defeat of the Third Reich and the evil it embodied, life in Britain did not immediately return to pre-war normality. Instead, severe rationing remained in effect. While no one would wish for the conflict to resume, everyday life was full of hardships and deprivations and many Britons endured lives still echoing the dreariness of wartime but with none of the drama.

A welcome distraction from this seemingly endless postwar austerity was provided by the Royal Family when, on July 9, 1947, the announcement came from Buckingham Palace heralding the engagement of Her Royal Highness The Princess Elizabeth to Lieutenant Philip Mountbatten, RN. The wedding — on November 20 of that same year — was described by wartime Prime Minister Sir Winston Churchill as "a flash of colour on the hard road we have to travel."

At ages twenty-six and twenty-one respectively, Philip and Elizabeth were the Charles and Diana of their era on their wedding day, according to their cousin, the Countess Mountbatten of Burma. Recalling the excitement surrounding the royal wedding sixty years later, the Countess said, "If you think in terms of the Prince of Wales and Diana, it was exactly the same. I mean, they were the sorts of star personalities and it was the first time television was being used and they were, absolutely, stars. And everybody was very happy … for the Princess to find such a nice husband. Everybody was rejoicing."

Clement Attlee's Labour Government did not declare November 20, 1947, a national holiday, but

Princess Elizabeth and the Duke of Edinburgh exchange loving looks while posing for their wedding photograph. The wedding was "a flash of colour" in the postwar years.

this refusal did not prevent thousands from camping out on the streets of London in an effort to secure a view of the wedding procession and millions more around the world from listening to the ceremony on the wireless and devouring wedding coverage featured in newspapers, magazines, and newsreels. A fortunate few were able to watch the ceremony on television. By mid-October — nearly a month before the wedding — one spectator seat along the route had sold for £3,000, while one room in Whitehall had been rented for nearly £4,000.

Documents recently released by the National Archives in London demonstrate both the enthusiasm of ordinary people for the wedding and the concerns of the Palace and branches of government regarding the production of wedding souvenirs. While Palace courtiers seemed to be most worried about poor taste, the government was uneasy about the impact on Britain's weakened industrial base of producing impractical trinkets, such as flags and handkerchiefs bearing likenesses of the royal couple. However, public demand prevailed

and royal wedding mementos were produced, to the delight of the majority of the British public. Although central London would not be floodlit, the Princess's trousseau would be less lavish than that of her mother, and fewer banners would be hung farther apart on lampposts along the wedding route, the wedding was still an impressive example of royal pageantry at its best. The public was treated to a spectacle worthy of a fairy tale and the stage was set for the Princess's life as a beloved — and very visible — future monarch.

Not since the funeral of King Edward VII in 1910 had so many members of royal houses near and far converged on London. Although rationing was still in effect, foreign royals threw off the shackles of wartime austerity, and the finest suites in London's finest hotels were soon filled with crowned heads and their royal retinues. The guest list included the King and Queen of Denmark; the King and Queen of Yugoslavia; the Kings of Iraq, Norway, and Romania; the Queen Mother of Romania; the Queen of the Hellenes; the Belgian Prince Regent;

A cake stand depicting the royal couple was one example of the less expensive wedding commemoratives.

ELIZABETH AND PHILIP

NOV. 20 1947

SOUVENIR OF THE

ROYAL WEDDING

AT WESTMINSTER ABBEY
ON NOVEMBER 20th 1947

A C.R.C. PRODUCTION

2/6

Princess Juliana, the Regent of the Netherlands, and her consort, Prince Bernhardt; the grand ducal family of Luxembourg; the deposed royal family of Spain; and Queen Salote of Tonga.

Philip's sisters — married to Germans — were not invited to the ceremony but sent him a gold pen engraved with their names as a wedding gift. His devoutly religious mother, Princess Alice of Greece, set aside her nun's habit and wimple and donned a lace gown and matching hat in honour of the occasion. In spite of the outlaw status of her daughters and their spouses, Princess Alice had earned her place in Westminster Abbey, and not merely as the groom's mother. Rather, she had demonstrated goodness and courage during the war, as she had hidden a Jewish family in her Athens home during the German occupation of Greece. Years after her death, her son accepted a posthumous award for her valour from the state of Israel. The Duke and Duchess of Windsor, formerly King Edward VIII and Wallis Simpson, who shared a reputation of self-interest during the Second World War, were also left off the invitation list. They spent the wedding day in America.

The bride's day began with a cup of tea brought to her by her faithful and formidable dresser,

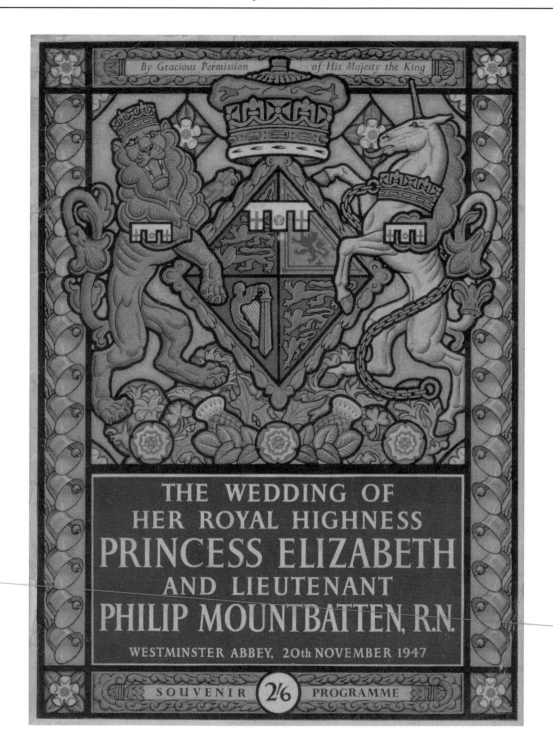

A beautiful Princess Elizabeth poses in her magnificent wedding dress.

Miss Margaret "Bobo" MacDonald. According to the ever-present Marion "Crawfie" Crawford, the bride's former governess, Princess Elizabeth, in her dressing gown, peeped excitedly out her windows at the crowds who had camped out in the bitterly cold weather, fifty people deep in some places.

According to Crawfie's account, the excited bride-to-be told her, "I can't believe it's really happening. I have to keep pinching myself."

The bride's dress had been personally delivered the night before by its creator, Norman (later Sir Norman) Hartnell. Hartnell had been responsible for the romantic wardrobe adopted by Princess Elizabeth's mother, Queen Elizabeth, when King George VI ascended to the Throne. One of the dresses, famously worn by her in a photographic portrait by Cecil Beaton, is both romantic and regal, a feat he was to repeat with this, the wedding dress of a future queen. Although rationing was still in effect, the Princess was allotted one hundred extra clothing coupons towards the creation of her wedding gown, and so the dress did not visibly reflect any postwar dreariness. The secrecy surrounding its creation made its eventual unveiling even more exciting. Workers at Hartnell's studio all signed confidentiality agreements and workroom windows were whitewashed and covered with thick white muslin to further ensure privacy.

The dress — inspired by Botticelli's painting *Primavera* — was made of ivory satin and tulle and embroidered with more than ten thousand seed pearls patterned as white roses of York entwined with ears of corn embroidered in crystal. The dress and train also featured other embroidered flower motifs: syringa, jasmine, and wheat ears among them. The dress took two months of work by twenty-five needlewomen and ten embroiderers to complete. The Princess's shoes were matching peep-toed satin slingbacks with high heels by royal shoemaker Edward Rayne. The eight bridesmaids — led by Princess Margaret and including Princess Alexandra of Kent and Lord Mountbatten's daughter, Lady Pamela Mountbatten — were also dressed by Hartnell. Cleverly, each of these dresses featured a large satin bow at the bodice, but the gowns were constructed largely of unrationed net material and embroidered with tiny stars. Even so, the bridesmaids also used all of their clothing rations for these very special dresses. The fabulous Russian tiara given to her by her grandmother, Queen Mary, anchored the Princess's tulle veil. Often worn by Queen Elizabeth II throughout her reign, this tiara features a series of graduated spikes, each of which is composed of diamonds arranged by size.

The tiara was featured in one of the last-minute glitches that seem to plague most weddings, from the humble to the grand. The wedding of Elizabeth and Philip was not immune. As the tiara was being placed on the Princess's head (her hair having been styled earlier by the prominent hairdresser Monsieur Henri) during the seventy-five-minute final fitting, it snapped in two. The tiara was soon repaired, but then it was found that the Princess's double-strand pearl necklace — a wedding gift from her parents — was not in her dressing room at Buckingham Palace but rather at St. James's Palace displayed with the couple's other wedding gifts. Elizabeth's recently appointed private secretary, Jock Colville, came to the rescue and retrieved the pearls in time, but only after commandeering and then jettisoning the car carrying King Haakon VII of Norway and embarking on a harrowing journey by foot through the crowds gathered around both palaces! The bride's bouquet had gone missing as well. Fortunately, a full search of Buckingham Palace was cut short when a helpful footman revealed he had put the flowers in an icebox in an effort to properly preserve them.

Although the Princess glittered in her wedding finery, she was, of course, unable to wear all of the jewels she had received as wedding gifts. Her parents had also given her a sapphire and diamond suite of necklace and earrings and a pair of Cartier

A diamond and ruby necklace was one of the wedding gifts given to Princess Elizabeth by her parents, the King and Queen.

The Canadian gift for the Duke of Edinburgh was wood panelling in white Canadian maple for his study at Clarence House.

diamond chandelier earrings, among other jewellery. Coincidentally, the geometric style of the earrings was reminiscent of Philip's wedding gift to his bride — a diamond bracelet he had designed himself. Philip had also designed the couple's gifts to their bridesmaids — tiny gold compacts with the initials "E&P" traced in jewels. Queen Mary gave her granddaughter not only the Russian tiara but also more spectacular and sentimental pieces of jewellery, including an antique diamond stomacher, Indian bangle brooches studded with diamonds and meant for an empress, and the ruby earrings King George V had given her for her fifty-ninth birthday. Other gifts of jewellery included rubies from the people of Burma, a 54.5-carat uncut pink diamond from the Canadian tycoon John T. Williamson, a diamond tiara and bandeau from the Nizam of Hyderabad, and an emerald and diamond necklace from the people of Victoria, British Columbia. With diamonds from his mother's tiara, Philip gave his bride a brooch in the shape of a Royal Navy badge.

The nearly three thousand wedding gifts the couple received included a racehorse, a twenty-two-carat gold coffee service, a hunting lodge in Kenya, and a television set. From Canada, Elizabeth received a mink coat and the couple received maple furniture for their country home and wall panelling for Philip's study in Clarence House. The newlyweds received a striking Chinese dinner service — featuring orange dragons — from President Chiang Kai Shek, a Steuben crystal bowl engraved with a merry-go-round from President Truman on behalf of the American people, and, most famously, a square of cloth with a fringe woven by Mahatma Gandhi. Princess Margaret reportedly hid this piece of cloth from Queen Mary, who mistook it for a loincloth and declared it "such an indelicate gift." This legendary but humble offering was displayed among grander gifts as part of a special exhibition in England celebrating the Queen and the Duke of Edinburgh's sixtieth wedding anniversary held in the summer of 2007. Touchingly, the Princess also received 386 pairs of precious nylon stockings — many of them from ordinary young women her age.

The groom had promised his bride that he would quit smoking. He kept this promise but did indulge in a pre-wedding gin and tonic with his best man and cousin, David, Marquess of Milford Haven. Dashing

Among the other Canadian gifts was a silver tea service from British Columbia, displayed by the province's Agent-General, W.A. McAdam, and Mrs. McAdam.

in his naval uniform and carrying a ceremonial sword that had belonged to his grandfather, Prince Louis of Battenberg, Philip, who was admired as a war veteran and viewed by the public not as a foreign prince but instead as a "real man," could be forgiven any pre-wedding nerves as he made his way from Kensington Palace — through the excited throngs filling the streets — to Westminster Abbey, where more than two thousand guests would gather.

The procession to the Abbey was glittering and grand. Both the heralds and the Household Cavalry were kitted out in full ceremonial dress, which had

Princess Elizabeth arrives at Westminster Abbey.

not been unearthed since before the war. The many distinguished guests returned to pre-war sartorial grandeur as the kings, queens, princesses, rajahs, dukes and duchesses, earls and countesses took their jewels out of safekeeping and wore them to the wedding. The Countess Mountbatten of Burma recalls that female guests wore long gowns (which required extra material) with their obligatory hats at the daytime wedding — another departure from wartime utility.

Queen Mary led the procession to the Abbey, sitting upright in her Daimler, followed by plume-helmeted Life Guards. Queen Elizabeth and Princess Margaret followed, the Queen waving happily, true to form. The Horse Guards followed Philip's car, and then the bride and the King emerged to cheers and shouts of "God bless you!"

Arriving at Westminster Abbey in the Irish State Coach after this impressive procession, Princess Elizabeth — with her father beside her — was the focus of all eyes. Two seamstresses waited at the Abbey in case there were any problems with the Princess's dress and fifteen-foot train. The congregation was a colourful one. Not only did English aristocrats and European royals wear their finest jewels, but maharajahs wore their turbans, sheiks were in robes, and choir and clergy were outfitted in scarlet and snowy white, the

Prince William of Gloucester and Prince Michael of Kent, young cousins of Princess Elizabeth, served as pageboys.

cumulative effect grander than anything seen since before the war.

Philip and the Marquess of Milford Haven, having already entered through the Poet's Corner

Princess Elizabeth and the Duke of Edinburgh took their vows of marriage before the high altar of Westminster Abbey.

door, stood waiting. The Princess made her way down the carpeted aisle on her father's arm having made only one error: with two nervous young pageboys — Prince William of Gloucester and Prince Michael of Kent — holding her train, the Princess neglected to place her bouquet of orchids on the Tomb of the Unknown Warrior as her mother had done on her wedding day. As she walked up the aisle, she smiled, and she returned Philip's grin after he made a ceremonial bow to the King. The Dean of Westminster began the rite of solemnization and the Archbishop of Canterbury performed the ceremony, which was broadcast by the BBC throughout the world. The normal order of a Church of England service was followed, with the Princess promising to obey her husband, an ideal she could aspire to in her personal life but never in her monarchical role. The Princess's musical request was "The Lord Is My Shepherd," set to a traditional Scottish tune. Philip placed the ring — made of the same Welsh gold as her mother's wedding ring — on Elizabeth's finger. During the signing of the register, the

King, deeply moved, told the Archbishop, "It is a far more moving thing to give your daughter away than to be married yourself."

Noel Coward wrote in his diary of the wedding, "A gala day … the wedding was most moving and beautifully done. English tradition at its best." After the ceremony, the newly married couple bowed and

The newlyweds depart in the Glass Coach.

curtseyed to the King and Queen and travelled to Buckingham Palace in the Glass Coach waving and smiling, the first of many ceremonial journeys they would take together.

At the wedding breakfast, the King's teary-eyed but simple toast, "To the bride," only hinted at his strong emotions. On her honeymoon, the Princess received a letter from her father, which outlined his true feelings:

I was so proud of you & thrilled at having you so close to me on your long walk in Westminster Abbey, but when I handed your hand to the Archbishop I felt that I had lost something very precious. You were so calm & composed during the Service & said your words with such conviction, that I knew everything was all right....

I have watched you grow up all these years with pride under the skilful direction of Mummy, who, as you know, is the most marvellous person in the World in my eyes, & I can, I know, always count on you, & now Philip, to help us in our work. Your leaving has left a great blank in our lives but do remember that your old home is still yours & do come back to it as much & as often as possible. I can see that you are sublimely happy with Philip which is right but don't forget us is the wish of

Your ever loving & devoted
Papa.

The King's toast also served to underline the instructions he and the Queen had issued regarding the length of speeches at the celebration. Their memories of suffering through the musings of long-winded relatives on their own wedding day had made them determined to spare their daughter the same fate!

The bunches of white heather and myrtle sent down from Balmoral decorating the tables and the playing of the bagpipes set the tone for a festive gathering for the 150 guests, as did twelve wedding cakes. The official wedding cake, at nine feet tall, was anchored on the first tier by replicas of Windsor Castle, Buckingham Palace, and Balmoral (made of sugar), as well as the bride and groom's insignia. The second tier featured a rendering of the Princess taking the salute as Colonel of the Grenadier Guards, a night scene of the Battle of Matapan, and sporting motifs that reflected the couple's many interests. The third featured a cupid with initialed shields, ATS and Girl Guide badges, and a replica of the Duke's wartime ship, HMS *Valiant*. The last layer was crowned with symbols of the Commonwealth. The guests dined on fish and partridge. One of the guests, Princess Elizabeth's former governess, "Crawfie," wrote, "It was a gay and merry lunch party. The tables were decorated with smilax and white carnations, and at each of our places there was a little bunch of white heather, sent down from Balmoral. The famous gold-plate and the scarlet-coated footmen gave a fairy-tale atmosphere to it all, and I was in a veritable dream."

After two appearances on the palace balcony — another royal wedding tradition demanded by the public, the couple departed on their honeymoon.

Vast crowds greeted Elizabeth and Philip at the traditional balcony appearance following the wedding and the royal couple waved back.

The family photograph for the wedding.

open landau from Buckingham Palace to Waterloo Station. This chilly journey was designed with the public in mind. Elizabeth and Philip were warmed somewhat by hot water bottles and the Princess's favourite corgi, Susan. The King and Queen held hands as they saw the young couple off, and Princess Alice did not stop waving until their carriage disappeared from view. As the young couple drove by the joyful, cheering crowds on that cold, foggy day in London, they were a visible reminder that at least one fairy tale came true in a war-torn world.

Given the tenor of the times, a trip abroad was viewed as unacceptably extravagant, so the couple departed for two eventual destinations that held family links for each of them. Their first stop was Broadlands, the Mountbatten family home in Hampshire, followed by a stay at Birkhall, on the Royal Family's Balmoral estate in Scotland.

The bride's trousseau included a crepe dress with a blue velvet coat and a blue felt bonnet trimmed with ostrich feathers and curved twills in two tones of blue, which she wore as the couple set off for their honeymoon. As they were waved off and showered in rose petals by all at the palace — including their eight bridesmaids and two young pageboys — the royal couple travelled in an unheated

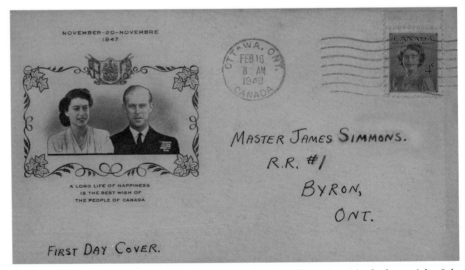

A Canadian first day cover declared that "A long life of happiness is the best wish of the People of Canada."

2 Paths to the Abbey

"This is no arranged marriage"
— *The Daily Mail*

Greece is the cradle of Western Civilization, but from the middle of the fifteenth century until the nineteenth century Greece languished under the yoke of the alien Ottoman Empire. Finally, after the Greek war of independence, which began in 1821, it gained its complete sovereignty and its first modern king, Otto I, in 1832. He was a Bavarian prince chosen by the great powers but, despite a promising start and a long reign, he became unpopular and was deposed in 1862.

In 1863 Prince William of Schleswig-Holstein-Sonderburg-Glucksburg, second son of King Christian IX of Denmark, was chosen as the new king, taking the name George I. He was the second choice, as the Greeks had asked Queen Victoria for her second son, Prince Alfred, Duke of Edinburgh. Victoria thought it was too unpredictable a situation for her son and put forward Prince William, who was the brother of her new daughter-in-law, Princess Alexandra, the Princess of Wales. He was acceptable to the Russians because there was a distant connection between the Glucksburgs and the Romanovs (and his sister Dagmar subsequently married the heir to the Russian throne and became the Empress of Russia). The Greeks, being pro-British since Britain had ceded to them the Ionian Islands, including Corfu, readily accepted Queen Victoria's choice.

The world was to come full circle. Prince Alfred eventually succeeded his uncle as Duke of Coburg in the German Empire, and after his death his British title, Duke of Edinburgh, reverted to the Crown. King George I's grandson Prince Philip of Greece, born at Mon Repos on Corfu, married Princess Elizabeth of Windsor and was granted the title of Duke of Edinburgh in 1947.

King George I, second monarch of independent Greece, founder of the modern Greek royal dynasty, and grandfather of Prince Philip.

Prince Andrew and Princess Alice of Greece, parents of Prince Philip, in 1906.

Both of royal blood, Elizabeth and Philip could not have had more different upbringings, yet they both emerged as individuals who were self-disciplined and dutiful.

Prince Philip was born on June 10, 1921. His father, Prince Andrew of Greece, was a younger son of King George I and a brother of King Constantine I. He was a lieutenant general in the Greek Army and, in 1922, was sentenced to perpetual banishment by the Greek Chamber of Deputies for his alleged role in the defeat of the Greeks by the Turks at the Battle of Smyrna. The monarchy, which was officially abolished in 1924, had been undermined by British and French intrigues during and after the First World War, and the charges against Prince Andrew were trumped up by the republicans who had taken control of the country, to cover up their own incompetence.

Philip's mother, Princess Alice, was the daughter of Prince Louis of Battenberg and Princess Victoria of Hesse, granddaughter of Queen Victoria. Prince Louis had lived most of his life in England, served in the Royal Navy, and risen to become First Sea Lord, the senior serving officer in the Fleet, by the start of the First World War. Solely because of his German name and inherited titles he was forced to resign his post by anti-German hysteria led by men such as H.G. Wells, who had claimed that even the King was "alien and uninspiring." George V replied, "I may be uninspiring but I'm damned if I'm alien." Neither he nor Prince Louis was either, but the King decided to change the royal name from Saxe-Coburg-Gotha to Windsor. His royal and princely relations in Britain, including the Battenbergs, were forced to comply as well. The Battenbergs became the Mountbattens, and Prince Louis gave up his German princely status

and was granted the English peerage of Marquess of Milford Haven. His elder son eventually succeeded him in his title. His younger son became Lord Louis Mountbatten, later Earl Mountbatten of Burma.

Prince Philip was his parents' fifth child and only son. His birthplace was a Regency-style villa that, perhaps prophetically, had been the residence of the British Commissioners in the days when Corfu was a British possession.

Prince Andrew, rescued from a firing squad by international intervention, with Princess Alice and their family, including Prince Philip, left Greece on a Royal Navy ship for Britain on December 3, 1922.

Mon Repos, on Corfu, was the birthplace of Prince Philip in 1921.

A young Prince Philip in the uniform of the Greek Royal Guard, the Evzones.

The family returned to the Continent and settled in Paris, living first in the Bois-de-Boulogne and then at Saint-Cloud, in homes that belonged to Marie Bonaparte, wife of Prince George, an elder brother of Prince Andrew. Prince Philip started his education at the Elms school in Saint-Cloud. At the age of eight

he returned to Britain and attended Cheam School in Surrey, from 1930 to 1933. In 1933 he attended Salem School in Baden, Germany, and in 1934 he went to Gordonstoun School near Elgin, Morayshire, in Scotland. Gordonstoun had been founded by Kurt Hahn, the former headmaster of Salem, who had been forced out of Germany by the Nazis.

Prince Philip's childhood was rootless and unsettled, without a homeland or even a surname. His parents apart — his mother ill and largely incommunicado in Switzerland and his father living in reduced circumstances in Monaco — he spent his youth under the wings of various members of his extended family. While living in Britain the Prince lived partly with his grandmother, Princess Victoria, in Kensington Palace and partly with his uncle, the 2nd Marquess of Milford Haven, at Lynden Manor near Maidenhead. Of the Prince's attitude regarding his childhood, his biographer, Gyles Brandreth, writes, "'It's simply what happened' is what Prince Philip says today in his characteristic matter-of-fact way. 'The family broke up. My mother was ill, my sisters were married, my father was in the South of France. I just had to get on with it. You do. One does.'"

Elizabeth II's royal journey also followed a circuitous and unexpected route. Her grandfather, King George V, was the younger son of King Edward VII. He had been the Duke of York and succeeded to the Throne only because his elder brother, Albert Victor, Duke of Clarence, had died. Princess May of Teck had been engaged to the Duke of Clarence but following his death married the Duke of York. In 1901, with his father becoming King, the Duke acquired the title Duke of Cornwall and York and then was created Prince of Wales. He became King upon his father's death in 1910.

Similarly Elizabeth II's father was not originally expected to be King either. Prince Albert, Duke of York, was the second son of King George V and bore the title originally held by his father as a second son. He married Lady Elizabeth Bowes-Lyon, daughter of the Earl and Countess of Strathmore and Kinghorne, in 1923.

Princess Elizabeth was born on April 21, 1926, at 17 Bruton Street in London, the home of her maternal grandparents. Although she was the third in line to the Throne at her birth, after her uncle the Prince of Wales and her father, the odds were against her becoming the Sovereign. She would be supplanted by any children born to her uncle and any sons that her parents might have, even though they would be younger than her. At the same time, however, the possibility was noted. The *Toronto Daily Star* commented, "There is a possibility that today's baby may become … Sovereign," and the next day, reflecting on the expectation that the child would be named Elizabeth, added, "Elizabeth makes a strong appeal to the popular imagination because of the possibility of the little newcomer some day ascending the Throne" and bringing "another Elizabethan era."

The Princess was named Elizabeth Alexandra Mary, after her mother, her great-grandmother Queen Alexandra, and her grandmother Queen Mary. She was baptized at the private chapel at Buckingham Palace on May 29, with water from the River Jordan. The chapel was destroyed on September 13, 1940, during a German bombing raid in the Second World War. Some twenty years

Souvenir wedding postcard of the Duke of York and Lady Elizabeth Bowes-Lyon (King George VI and Queen Elizabeth), parents of Princess Elizabeth.

The birthplace of Princess Elizabeth in 1926, 17 Bruton Street, the London home of her maternal grandparents, the Earl and Countess of Strathmore.

later, at the suggestion of Prince Philip, the site of the chapel was rebuilt as the Queen's Gallery, to share art from the Royal Collection with the general public, the first part of Buckingham Palace to be so accessible when it opened on July 25, 1962. It was redesigned and reopened in 2002 for the Queen's Golden Jubilee, and remains open as the site of frequent exhibits of all types of art, held in trust by the Queen.

As a princess, Elizabeth was raised in a loving family circle, albeit a formal one by contemporary

Marcus Adam's portrait photograph of Princess Elizabeth at age two.

standards, with an emphasis on self-control and good manners. Not born to be a queen, Elizabeth's upbringing was similar to that of other girls of her class and era. Educated at home, she and her sister were raised with the assistance of their Scottish governess, Marion Crawford, who stayed with them into adulthood. However, young Lilibet and Margaret Rose also saw their devoted and loving mother and father every day, except when their royal duties took them abroad. One such trip occurred in 1927, when Lilibet was only nine months old. The Duke and Duchess of York visited Australia and New Zealand, a trip that kept them away for six months. Royal duty in this case meant they missed their elder daughter's first birthday, first words, and first steps. However, even with their royal responsibilities, the Yorks spent more time with their daughters than many aristocratic parents of the period. They shunned a glittering social life in favour of a happy family life, and they gave their daughters as much time and attention as they could. When they were unable to do so, two sets of loving grandparents were able to act as substitutes.

The Princess acquired the pet name of "Lilibet" from her initial inability to say her name. Her grandfather, King George V, who adored her, took a liking to his granddaughter's version of her name and began calling her "Lilibet" himself. Soon the whole family followed suit. Like Prince Philip, Princess Elizabeth had several homes, but they were permanent residences — her parents' homes of 145 Picadilly Street in London, Royal Lodge in Windsor Great Park, and Birkhall in Scotland. In addition time was spent at her maternal grandparents' castle at Glamis and at her paternal grandparents' homes, which eventually became her parents' and then her own, at Buckingham Palace, Windsor Castle, and Balmoral.

While Princess Elizabeth's education took place at home, not in a school, her parents, and especially Queen Mary, ensured that she received thorough instruction in French, history, genealogy, and geography, with emphasis on the Commonwealth.

Although Elizabeth and Philip acquired their educations in vastly different manners, the results were remarkably similar in many fields. They both became fluent in several languages and experts in their knowledge of the culture, history, and institutions of the multicultural lands of which they would one day become Sovereign and Consort. A young French-Canadian reporter with separatist leanings once tried to be difficult by speaking French to the then Queen Elizabeth II, thinking this would upset her. Instead Her Majesty instantly switched into a fluent French conversation with her, completely winning the reporter over. On another occasion young Greek-Canadians in Toronto called out to the Prince in Greek during a walkabout, and the Prince impressed them by replying in Greek.

Two great constitutional developments occurred while Elizabeth and Philip were quite young. The first they would have hardly been aware of at the time. The second, for the Princess at least, was shocking and confusing. Both were to change the lives they would live.

In 1926, the year Princess Elizabeth was born, the Imperial Conference in London agreed that in the future each of the dominions of the King would be equal in status to the United Kingdom. Henceforth the King, for example, would be King of Canada in its own right and not just because it was part of the British Empire. It was the beginning of the Commonwealth. The decisions were given statutory constitutional effect with the Statute of Westminster in 1931. This decision would lead to the fact that Elizabeth and Philip would be Queen and Consort of sixteen separate monarchies in the year 2007. It would also mean that their lives together, first as Princess and Duke and then as Queen and Prince, would include travel to these scattered realms on a scale and frequency never before experienced by their ancestors or the monarchs of any other lands. It would be a different type of monarchy they would guide.

In 1930 Canada was searching for a new governor general. The new Canadian Government, led by R.B. Bennett, asked for the Duke of York to take the position. Though King George V and the Duke had their own reservations, as the Duke and Duchess had just added to their family with the

Rideau Hall in Ottawa almost became Princess Elizabeth's home in 1930. She first stayed there in 1951 and it became her official Canadian home in 1952.

birth of Princess Margaret and the King wanted the Duke close to compensate for the weaknesses he had already noted in his eldest son, the Canadians might have won them over had the discussions been between them and the King and Duke alone.

Unfortunately for Canadians 1930 fell in between the enunciation of the new status for Canada as a fully independent kingdom and its legal implementation in 1931, so the request had to be approved by the British Government. The Minister for the Dominions, the unimaginative J.H. Thomas, blocked the request, not because of the domestic concerns of the Royal Family but because, without any knowledge of Canada, he decided that Canadians did not like the Royal Family, despite the fact that the government elected by those Canadians felt otherwise. If the timing had been less than two years later the British Government would have had no say in the matter. As it was, its last act

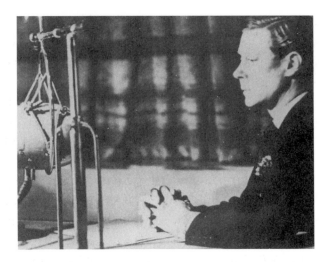

King Edward VIII announces his abdication, which changed Princess Elizabeth's life forever.

in the appointment of Canadian governors general was to prevent the future King of Canada and the future Queen of Canada from living in Canada before ascending to the Throne. Princess Elizabeth growing up at Rideau Hall in Ottawa remains one of the more intriguing might-have-beens in royal history. For Princess Elizabeth the rejection of the request meant twenty-one more years would pass before she saw Canada.

The second event, which would shake the foundations of the Monarchy itself, was the abdication of King Edward VIII to marry the twice-divorced American Wallis Simpson. On this issue all the Commonwealth governments were in agreement. Edward could not marry Wallis Simpson and remain King. Elizabeth and Philip were old enough to understand the significance of this development. Elizabeth, especially, knew what it meant for her, though at ten years old she naturally did not initially grasp what the crisis was about. Hearing bits and pieces of the dispute between the King and his Prime Minister, Stanley Baldwin, she explained to Princess Margaret, "I think Uncle David wants to marry Mrs Baldwin and Mr Baldwin doesn't like it." But when told that their uncle had abdicated she understood clearly the implications. Princess Margaret asked her sister if that meant she would one day become Queen. "Yes, some day," Princess Elizabeth replied.

The year 1936 was a significant one for both Princess Elizabeth and Prince Philip. In the Commonwealth it was the year of three kings. The year started with King George V on the Throne. The venerable old king died on January 20 and was succeeded by his eldest son, King Edward VIII, who abdicated on December 11 to be followed by his brother, King George VI. Princess Elizabeth had begun the year third in line to the Throne and ended it first in line. Meanwhile in Greece a plebiscite had restored its monarchy, and in November the bodies of Prince Philip's grandmother, Queen Olga, and his uncle and aunt, King Constantine I and Queen Sophie, who had all died in exile, were taken back to Greece for burial. Prince Philip and his father, Prince Andrew, were among the Greek royal family reunited in their homeland, and it was the younger prince's first royal ceremony. The following year Princess Elizabeth took part in the great Coronation ceremony of her parents, the first time that a monarch was crowned not only Sovereign of the United Kingdom but also of Canada, Australia, New Zealand, South Africa, and Ireland separately, each kingdom being named in the ceremony. In Greece that year Prince Philip took part in his second royal event, the wedding of Crown Prince Paul to Princess Frederika of Hanover, at which he was one of the three best men.

With Prince Philip together with his parents for the first time in many years, the question of his future was raised. With the restoration of the Greek monarchy some members of its royal family and the royalist government in power wished the young prince to return to Greece and enlist at the Greek Nautical College, and then follow a career in the Royal Hellenic Navy. Prince Philip declined the entreaties and returned to England for his final year at Gordonstoun and a career in the British Royal Navy.

At Gordonstoun he excelled at sports and physical activities, being captain of both the field hockey and cricket teams and a member of the

Prince Philip demonstrating his athletic prowess in cricket.

school's coast guard unit. He finished his time at the school as Head Boy. Kurt Hahn said of the Prince in his final report, "He has the greatest sense of service of all the boys in the school."

On the advice of his uncle, Lord Louis Mountbatten, he took the civil service exams and was accepted by the Royal Navy as a Special Entry Cadet at the Royal Naval College, Dartmouth, on May 1, 1939. Philip has said that his natural inclination was to join the air force, but he was encouraged by Lord Louis to join the navy in part because he would be following family tradition. At Dartmouth he earned the King's Dirk as best all-round cadet of his term and the Eardly-Howard-Crockett Prize for best cadet.

The first meeting of Princess Elizabeth and Prince Philip took place at the Royal Naval College at Dartmouth in July 1939, when the King, the Queen, and the Princesses Elizabeth and Margaret, accompanied by Philip's uncle Lord Louis Mountbatten, made an official visit. Philip, a cadet, was one of the few young men to come in contact with the young Princesses,

Princess Elizabeth at age seventeen.

due in part to an outbreak of the mumps within the ranks. This led to him spending much of the visit entertaining the Princesses.

In spite of a five-year age difference between Prince Philip and Princess Elizabeth — he was eighteen, she was thirteen — she became enamoured of the tall, handsome young man with his Nordic good looks and easy confidence. An account by the Princesses' indiscreet governess, Marion "Crawfie" Crawford, seems to confirm this theory: "I thought he showed off a great deal, but the little girls were much impressed. Lilibet said, 'How good he is, Crawfie. How high he can jump.' She never took her eyes off him the whole time."

Philip's seeming patience with having to entertain "the little girls" and his "showing off" seem to suggest that Princess Elizabeth's feelings did not go unreciprocated. And at the end of the Royal Family's visit, his was the last of the small boats to turn back as the royal yacht left the harbour. While watching Philip rowing furiously in an effort to keep up to the much larger *Victoria and Albert*, the King is said to have roared, "Damn young fool!" As the family sailed away, the seeds of a royal marriage had been planted.

Sixty years of successful marriage is proof that Elizabeth's early instincts were correct; that is, Philip was the man for her. However, not only did the couple encounter the usual familial obstacles in the run-up to their marriage, but events outside their influence also served to stall their courtship — particularly the advent of the Second World War. Elizabeth was obviously too young to marry Philip soon after their initial acquaintance. As well, the Princesses spent much of the war behind the walls of Windsor Castle while Philip served in the Royal Navy, making regular visits and anything resembling a traditional courtship impossible. The King, in the early days of the war, and dressed in the uniform of Admiral of the Fleet, summed up the ominous and uncertain future faced by all in the British Empire during his 1939 Christmas broadcast:

> I said to the man who stood at the Gate of the year, "Give me a light that I may tread safely into the unknown." And he replied, "Go out into the darkness, and put your hand into the Hand of God. That shall be better than light, and safer than a known way." May that Almighty Hand guide and uphold us all.

The Royal Family was first admired and later beloved for experiencing and enduring the war alongside their subjects. The King, who vowed never to wear civilian clothes until the war was over, paid unannounced visits to troops overseas and throughout Britain, sometimes accompanied by the Queen during the latter. The couple also comforted countless civilians whose families, friends, homes, and neighbourhoods fell victim to the bombing campaign that was the Blitz. When bombs hit Buckingham Palace and the chapel was destroyed, the heartbreaking toll of these visits prompted the Queen to say, "I'm glad we've been bombed. It makes me feel I can look the East End in the face." Their sincerity was apparent to most people. When the King and Queen made their way through yet another bomb-ravaged community, someone called out, "Thank God for a good King!," to which the

Princess Elizabeth with troops in Brighton during the Second World War.

King replied, "Thank God for a good people!"

The Princesses' wartime residency at Windsor Castle was not merely a reprieve purchased by privilege. In both Norway and Holland, the British Government noted that the Nazis had made "a desperate effort" to capture members of those countries' royal families. With this in mind, the government strongly suggested that Elizabeth and Margaret be sent to Canada or the United States where they (and the future of the Crown) would be safe. If the young Princesses were captured, it was thought that the pressure on the King and Queen would be unbearable. The King and Queen refused, and like 1.5 million other children in England, the Princesses were moved to the presumed safety of the country for the duration of the war, even though many of their aristocratic peers were sent by their concerned parents to safe havens across the Atlantic. The Queen further strengthened the bond between the Royal Family and their subjects when she famously declared, "The children won't go

Prince Philip, age nineteen, about to board an airplane.

without me. I won't leave the King. And the King will never leave."

On April 25, 1942, Princess Elizabeth registered under the wartime youth service scheme, and in 1945, aged nineteen, she joined the Auxiliary Territorial Service (ATS), where she learned to drive and service various vehicles. Although the war ended before she could make use of her new skills, her time with the ATS was valuable, allowing her to experience life (albeit a somewhat sanitized version) in the world outside Windsor Castle and to potentially "do her bit" for the war effort.

Philip's war experience was far different from that of his future wife. From January 1940, he served in the Indian Ocean as a midshipman escorting Australian transports to the Mediterranean. He joined his first battleship, *Valiant*, in Egypt, where his squadron sank several Italian warships. Later, several ships in his squadron were destroyed by the Germans, a fate his ship narrowly escaped. As one of the youngest lieutenants in the Royal Navy, Philip was transferred back to Britain, where, as second in command in the destroyer *Wallace*, he served on convoy duty up and down the east coast of Britain in an area nicknamed "E-boat Alley," a tough and unrelenting assignment. His ship also covered the landing by the 1st Canadian Division in Sicily. Philip concluded the war with service in the Far East. He was mentioned in despatches, a well-deserved accolade that later helped to endear him to his future wife's subjects.

In spite of wartime and familial restrictions on their romance, Elizabeth had never forgotten her prince. In a letter to Crawfie in 1942, she mentioned Philip as "the one." In 1943, he and his cousin David

Milford Haven spent Christmas and New Year's with the Royal Family, and this only served to strengthen the Princess's devotion and resolve. Although the King and Queen did not object to Philip as marriage material for their beloved daughter, they had two rather sensible concerns. First, they felt Elizabeth was too young to marry, and second, because of the war, they felt she hadn't really experienced the normal, carefree life that many young people enjoy. War had curtailed the parties and dances that would have made up the social life of a young princess in peacetime. When the Princesses were able to briefly mix — incognito — with the rejoicing crowds on VE Day, the King wrote in his diary, "Poor darlings, they have never had any fun yet." Like all good parents, the King and Queen were also concerned that their daughter make a happy marriage — divorce, of course, was out of the question — and so they wanted to ensure that Philip was "the one," as Elizabeth had not had the opportunity to meet many other young men with whom to compare him.

To this end, they introduced the Princess to other worthy candidates, many of them eminently suitable members of the aristocracy. They also had both Princess Elizabeth and Princess Margaret accompany them on a postwar tour of South Africa in February 1947, a visit that had been a year in the planning. However, Princess Elizabeth had made up her mind and was quietly determined to marry. When Philip proposed informally to Lilibet in the summer of 1946 at Balmoral, she accepted. However, the engagement between the couple was not made public until almost a year later, on July 9, 1947, when an announcement was issued by Buckingham Palace:

Lieutenant Philip Mountbatten in 1947 as a lecturer at the Petty Officers' Training School at Corsham, Wilts.

It is with greatest pleasure that The King and Queen announce the betrothal of their dearly beloved daughter The Princess Elizabeth to Lieutenant Philip Mountbatten, RN, son of the late Prince Andrew of Greece and Princess Andrew (Princess Alice of Battenberg), to which union The King has gladly given his consent.

The delay in announcing the engagement was not due to any serious misgivings regarding Philip on the part of the King or the Queen. Instead, the King was reluctant to let his daughter go, and as concerned and loving parents, the royal couple thought a longer engagement period prudent.

Once the engagement was announced, the young couple catapulted into royal duty, beginning

This charcoal engagement sketch of Princess Elizabeth and Lieutenant Philip Mountbatten by Reed, a Canadian artist, was distributed by George Weston Limited of Canada.

with their appearance at a palace garden party the next day. Elizabeth's engagement ring was made up of stones belonging to Philip's mother. As her son could not afford a suitable engagement ring, Princess Alice had sent him her favourite tiara from Athens, with the intention that it be broken up, the stones used to create an engagement ring for Princess Elizabeth. In the end, eleven stones were used for the ring. This, along with any other bit of news surrounding the impending nuptials, captured the imagination of a global audience.

While the Princess and the public rejoiced, some courtiers bristled at Philip's ancestry and his independent and outspoken nature. However, although his rootless childhood had been far less sheltered and regimented than that of Princess

Elizabeth, he was no less a royal. As a great-great-grandson of Queen Victoria, a second cousin to King George VI, and related to the royal families of Russia, Prussia, Denmark, and Greece, Philip's royal status could not seriously be questioned. And although he had grown up without a homeland, he had a powerful ally in his uncle, Lord Louis Mountbatten.

Although some viewed Philip's romance with Elizabeth as the result of Mountbatten's "pushiness," the marriage of Philip and Elizabeth was an unarranged love match. The characteristics that made some courtiers question Philip's suitability were the very traits that Elizabeth found attractive and that her father generally respected. A royal version of a self-made man, Philip's independence, lack of pretension, and successful naval career ensured that he would instinctively understand the royal rules of conduct, yet be able to withstand the pressures of court and retain his individuality. Seen initially as a rough diamond, he was, in the eyes of the Royal Family, a diamond nevertheless and a suitable match for their daughter and the future Queen. On the eve of his wedding, Philip was created a Knight of the Garter by his future father-in-law. The following morning he was, in the words of King George VI, "created a Royal Highness and the titles of his peerage will be Baron Greenwich, Earl of Merioneth and Duke of Edinburgh."

The King said, "It is a lot to give a man at once, but I know Philip understands his responsibilities on his marriage to Lilibet."

Even the tabloids of the day approved of the match, with the *Daily Mail* stating bluntly, "This is no arranged marriage."

3
Bittersweet Pageant of Royal Weddings

"... the hall at Buckingham Palace was full of people; they cheered again and again"
— *Queen Victoria on her wedding day*

Marriages loom larger for a Crown obliged to perpetuate itself than for the ordinary run of humanity. Princess Elizabeth and Prince Philip's wedding in November 1947 was the latest episode in an absorbing, ongoing human drama of royal betrothals and nuptials. It had been unfolding for well over a thousand years, seldom with predictable, let alone predictably happy, results. Royal weddings have changed constantly, reflecting the customs and fashions of the times, the characters and peculiarities of the principal performers, the things common to marriage, the requirements of royalty. Though thinking but the thoughts of time, every royal bride and groom is a new performer on the stage, and therefore each royal marriage is to that extent unique.

It is the older generations of a family that keep its past alive. Elizabeth and Philip both had relations eager to recall to them marriages from an era that seemed more distant and exotic than it was because of the cataclysmic transformation of society by two world wars. Princess Elizabeth knew three of Queen Victoria's children: Prince Arthur, the Duke of Connaught; Princess Louise; and Princess Beatrice. The young Heiress Presumptive to the Throne loved history, so it would be surprising had she not absorbed some of her venerable relatives' tales of past royal nuptials, the great matrimonials of the Victorian age. These old relatives put life into the paintings of wedding ceremonies of yore that Elizabeth and Philip saw covering palace and castle walls. The bride's parents, King George VI and Queen Elizabeth, had their cherished wedding day at Westminster Abbey on April 23, 1923, to recollect too. Theirs was the first marriage of a prince in the ancient Abbey in over five hundred years, and more than a million people lined the streets to glimpse the bride and groom. Like the 1947 wedding, it took place in postwar austerity, hence was flowerless,

Princess Elizabeth was a bridesmaid at the marriage of Prince George, Duke of Kent, and Princess Marina of Greece at Westminster Abbey 1934. It was her first major royal occasion.

capital of the small German Grand Duchy of Hesse, forty-four years before Elizabeth's and his. Alice's, it is true, was a wedding that failed to achieve its promise, but it was nonetheless remembered with fond nostalgia as one of the last great royal gatherings of the pre-1914 world. No less than three ceremonies were required for the couple: a civil, a Lutheran, and an Orthodox. Led by the Russian Emperor, the royal guests at the wedding ambushed the Wolseley motor car carrying the bride and groom, briefly pelting it with rice and satin slippers as they departed for their honeymoon.

Princess Elizabeth by 1947 had experienced her share of family weddings. In 1934 one of her first public duties, at age eight, was to act as bridesmaid at the wedding of her uncle Prince George, the handsome, artistic, but hitherto licentious Duke of Kent, to the ravishing and stylish Princess Marina of Greece — "that dazzling pair," the couple was popularly dubbed. The Kents' wedding took place

Princess Marina leaving Buckingham Palace for the Abbey.

and served too as a welcome pause for an Empire mourning its myriad dead and trying desperately to recover normality.

Philip, for his part, though less encumbered by relatives, must have heard his mother, Princess Alice, allude to her own happy autumn wedding, when she espoused Prince Andrew of Greece at Darmstadt,

at Westminster Abbey on a cold, gloomy November day. Prior to it, the bride asked people to give money they would have used for presents for her to the unemployed and their children, for the world was writhing in the Great Depression. The Kents' wedding cake was made from Empire products and currants from Greece.

Duke and Duchess of Gloucester's wedding photograph with Princess Elizabeth as bridesmaid seated at lower left in her specially shortened dress.

Princess Elizabeth was a bridesmaid for the next major royal marriage too the following year, that of her uncle the Duke of Gloucester to Lady Alice Montagu-Douglas-Scott. The Princess wore a Hartnell dress of stiffened white tulle that, by command of her doting grandfather, King George V, was shortened to allow her pretty little knees to be seen. The Gloucesters' wedding would have been as splendid as the Kents' had not the bride's father less than three weeks before, causing the public ceremony to be cancelled in favour of a private rite at Buckingham Palace Chapel.

The person most keenly interested, most knowledgeable about family matrimonial occasions, was Princess Elizabeth's grandmother, the formidable Queen Mary, who could tell her granddaughter a strange tale of royal nuptials herself. Queen Mary exercised a formative influence on her granddaughter Elizabeth, inculcating in her a proper sense of royal duty, making sure that a thorough knowledge of the countries of the Empire was part of her curriculum. The events of Queen Mary's own marriage are a Cinderella story without the romance. Born Princess May of Teck, she belonged on her mother's side to a junior and impoverished branch of the Royal Family descended from King George III's seventh son, the Duke of Cambridge.

Popularly known as the people's princess, Princess May's mother, the fat, high-spirited but extravagant Princess Mary Adelaide of Cambridge, who struggled with debt, poverty, and the slights that go with them, in addition to a feckless husband, had ambitions for her daughter. Perhaps hardened by this challenging background, May turned into an intelligent, attractive, solid young woman of steady

Wedding of Elizabeth's II grandparents, King George V and Queen Mary (top right). The bride, Princess May, was first engaged to Prince Albert Victor, Duke of Clarence (above). When he unexpectedly died she wed his brother. Popular support for the marriage shown by this Punch cartoon (right) was a factor in its accomplishment.

"HYMEN HYMENÆE!"

character. Queen Victoria concluded that she would make an excellent wife for her grandson, Prince Albert Victor, Duke of Clarence and Avondale. Prince Eddy, as he was known, was second in line to the Throne, the eldest son of Prince Albert Edward, the Prince of Wales. He was an unsteady young man with problems. Lethargic, volatile, unstable, and dissipated, he could be described at best as a late developer. A stint in the Royal Navy with his younger brother Prince George had not improved him. Princess May's mother, dreaming that it was a chance to restore her family's fortunes, seized upon the marriage scheme and agreed with the Prince and Princess of Wales that May was just the strong-minded princess to help Eddy mature.

Not being passionate by nature, but having a great reverence for the grandeur of the Crown, May did not insist on romance in marriage and was ready to accept and share with the Prince the Throne he would inherit. Urged on by his parents, Prince Eddy proposed and was accepted in December 1891. Just over a month later he suddenly developed pneumonia and quietly died. His death probably saved his fiancée from marital misfortune, for as she had come to know Prince Eddy better Princess May had begun to have serious doubts about the wisdom of marrying him. In the widespread shock the Prince's unexpected death occasioned, newspapers raised the suggestion that Princess May would make an excellent bride for the remaining brother, Prince George of Wales.

Neither George nor May was in love with the other. George had recently proposed to and been rejected by his first cousin, Princess Marie of Edinburgh. After a year of mourning and grappling with the embarrassment she felt at being handed from the dead brother to the living, May accepted when Prince George finally put the question to her in the garden at Sheen Lodge, where he had taken her to look at the frogs in the pond. The wedding, when it took place at the Chapel Royal of St. James's Palace on July 6, 1893 — with the bride in silver and white brocade, presents (including a cow) to the value of over £1 million piling up in the Tecks' hitherto straitened household at White Lodge, and the London *haut monde* in a whirl — was the outcome of an unusual set of circumstances, but it was not unique. In the chequered saga of royal marriages, everything has usually happened before, and this was no exception, though Henry VIII's marriage to Katherine of Aragon, the widow of his deceased brother, Prince Arthur, nearly four centuries earlier, was hardly an auspicious precedent.

Different as Victorian weddings were to Elizabeth and Philip's, those of an earlier period undoubtedly surpassed them in the archaic. The Tudor Queen Mary I, the royal line's first Queen Regnant, was wed (temporarily, as it turned out) by proxy at age two and a half to the Dauphin of France, being held in the arms of her nurse for the ceremony, at which a ring was placed on her finger. In 1100 the wedding of King Henry I at Westminster Abbey to the daughter of Malcolm III Canmore, King of Scots, had a genealogical motivation. Princess Matilda, the bride, was originally named Edith, and her mother was Saint Margaret, a Saxon princess. It was wise policy, King Henry I felt, to introduce the Saxon royal blood into the Norman dynasty to consolidate its hold on the conquered English.

The manner and place of royal weddings varied considerably. Mary I's wedding, for at nearly forty she married Philip II of Spain, was held at Winchester Cathedral. James I's daughter Elizabeth, the "Winter Queen," married Frederick V, Elector Palatine, in the Chapel Royal of Whitehall Palace on Saint Valentine's Day in 1612. A secret nuptial mass dictated by the political climate followed Charles II's public Anglican wedding to a dowdy but decent Portuguese princess. The future Mary II's wedding with William III — the orange and the lemon, their Jacobite enemies named them — took place in her bedroom at St. James's Palace. St. Petersburg's Winter Palace provided a gorgeous setting for the Russian Orthodox marriage of Alfred, Duke of Edinburgh (second son of Queen Victoria), to the Grand Duchess Marie Alexandrovna in 1874, the bride wearing Russian court dress with an ermine and crimson velvet mantle. Afterwards followed the aesthetically more subdued Anglican marriage office performed by the Dean of Westminster, who was imported to the Russian capital for the occasion. For princesses marrying foreign royalty and departing to live in a far land, the process could be reversed. George II's daughter, Princess Mary, had a proxy marriage in 1740 at St. James's Palace but her actual wedding to the Landgrave of Hesse was a Calvinist rite in Cassel in Germany.

Centuries of dynastic nuptials created royal wedding procedures, customs, and traditions, many still in place in 1947 and remaining so today. Until the beginning of the nineteenth century, if the wedding involved foreign royalty, there was likely to be a proxy marriage followed by the actual ceremony when the bride or groom arrived. After the wedding came a showing of the married couple to the Court, officers of state, great nobles, and Members of

At the Duke of Kent's marriage in 1934, a private Russian Orthodox religious ceremony followed the Anglican.

Parliament. In the eighteenth century this was called the Nuptial Drawing Room. A banquet was also usually held. Oddities sometimes crept in, of course. At Frederick, Duke of York's espousal of Princess Frederica of Prussia in 1791 in Berlin, everyone sat down and played cards before the banquet. The same Duke of York was married in a general's full dress scarlet tunic because the great wars of the French Revolution and the Napoleonic era had just begun, and this started the custom still observed of royal princes being married in uniform.

Wedding trips and honeymoons, though an expected feature in 1947, were a recent addition to the royal marriage ritual. In earlier times the ceremony ended with the bride and groom being viewed together in bed by the Court. This custom, embarrassing to generations of brides but lasting into the eighteenth century, often led to bawdy exchanges. "So nephew, to your work! Hey Saint George for England," the lusty Charles II urged the groom, the dour William of Orange, at his niece Mary's bedding. In retrospect his gibe was ironic because neither Charles nor William succeeded in fathering a child in marriage.

Used as the modern world is to marriages of heirs to the Throne, not all kings and queens succeeded to the Crown married. Because of its rarity it is often forgotten that a number of sovereigns wed after they became monarchs. Some even did the unheard-of thing and never married at all. Queen Elizabeth I replied to the House of Commons when it asked her to marry that "in the end, this shall be for me sufficient that a marble stone shall declare that a Queen, having reigned such a time, lived and died a virgin." Her unmarried state needless to say was not from want of suitors. Edward VIII in the mid-twentieth century was another bachelor sovereign, though scarcely one pledged to virginity. He would likely have benefited from an arranged, dynastic marriage. It was his stubborn intention to wed an American double divorcee, unacceptable to the Commonwealth, that precipitated his abdication. When he did marry, his wedding was a plain civil one in a borrowed French château and he was no longer a king. The overwhelming majority of monarchs, however, agreed with King James I that "where there is no hope of succession, it breeds contempt and disdain," and so they married.

The Monarch whose place in history is assured by his marriages is of course Elizabeth and Philip's larger-than-life collateral ancestor, Henry VIII, who went through no fewer than six wedding ceremonies. Elizabeth and Philip's great-great-great-great-grandfather King George III took his bride, Princess Charlotte of Mecklenburg-Strelitz in Germany, a year after becoming King but prior to being crowned. He was an eager young man, and his marriage was a hurried affair; the bride reached St. James's Palace the day after her arrival from the Continent and was married at ten o'clock the same night. Ten bridesmaids, the unmarried daughters of dukes and earls, bore the train of her wedding dress. "Courage, Princess, courage," said her brother-in-law-to-be, the Duke of York, when he saw her tremble. But Charlotte was made of stern stuff; she was to bear George III fifteen children. After the wedding, ignoring fatigue, she attended the Nuptial Drawing Room with the Royal Family, where she sat down and played the harpsichord and sang to the guests. At the wedding ceremony itself every eye was on the nuptial crown George III gave his bride. Set with large jewels, it had a unique feature, four golden rods springing from the junction of the arches with a large solitaire diamond hanging from the end of each. The groom was dressed all in glittering silver fabric. To the Archbishop of Canterbury's question, Charlotte answered in mixed German and English, "Ich will."

Frequently expressed between the announcement of Elizabeth and Philip's engagement and their wedding was relief that the couple's was a love match. The general feeling was that it was a contemporary marriage, whereas arranged marriages were coercive, making the parties miserable for life. Besides the public's general aversion to foreign brides and grooms, it was the success of Elizabeth's parents' union that engendered such a conviction, a success that popularized another idea, too: it was easy for a non-royal to fit into the Royal Family. Elizabeth and Philip in the years ahead would discover that such an outlook, however modern, was naive and over-simplified to say the least. Love matches are just as likely to go on the rocks as arranged ones.

The Commonwealth, if truth be told, got the best of both worlds in the 1947 wedding. The future Queen married for love, but the man she loved possessed all the assets of a spouse of the old arranged matches. Despite the fiction that he was plain Lieutenant Mountbatten, Philip was a royal prince — a double prince, in fact. Belonging by birth to both Greek and Danish royal families, he

At Queen Charlotte's marriage in 1761 every eye focused on her stunning nuptial crown (left), a present from the groom, King George III. A Russian wedding crown with 1,535 diamonds (right) was worn by Queen Victoria's granddaughter Princess Alix of Hesse at her marriage to Emperor Nicholas II of Russia.

came from within the extended family circle and he knew the royal ropes. He endowed his descendants too with as representative a royal ancestry as the most sanguine chronicler of an arranged match could have hoped for. Was it his instinctive grasp of the situation that led Prince Philip to declare repeatedly that he was not a romantic?

The practice of making or cementing alliances, acquiring territory through heiresses, enhancing the Crown's prestige, flattering national aspirations, or uniting two (or more) peoples by a royal marriage was as old as kingship itself. Princess Elizabeth and Prince Philip were fortunate not to be pawns in such a game, but only when the political role of royalty was replaced by more routine constitutional, symbolic, and social functions had such considerations receded.

Although it was an arranged alliance, King George III's marriage was, like that of his descendants Elizabeth II and Prince Philip, mostly happy. But there is no doubt that the King was surprised — as the bride and groom in arranged marriages often are — when he first set eyes on the woman who would be his royal partner for life. It is now realized that cryptic allusions made by contemporaries to Queen Charlotte's appearance, especially those emphasizing her exceptionally wide nostrils, refer to the fact that her features had a strongly suggestive African cast. Scholars are convinced that Charlotte had black blood through her Portuguese ancestors. Many noticed the signs in her face at the time but with prevailing racial attitudes no one wished to say so openly. Once, the mother of a royal bride was even more shocked by the sight of the groom than was her daughter. "A monster!" was the

reaction of Queen Caroline, consort of George II, to Prince William of Orange when he came to St. James's Palace to marry Princess Anne, the Princess Royal, in 1734, for poor William was a hunchback. Fortunately, the Princess herself was quite content and fell happily in love with him.

Thankfully Elizabeth and Philip were spared the covens of witches that tried to frustrate the marriage their forbear James I arranged for himself with the Danish Princess Anne, a tall, shapely, Scandinavian blond beauty. James, called the wisest fool in Christendom by a wit of the period, was King of Scotland but soon to inherit the English and Irish crowns as well and become ancestor of both the Stuart and Hanoverian monarchs. According to the practice of the day, Princess Anne of Denmark was married to a royal proxy and set sail in 1589 for Scotland and her impatient groom. But fierce, unrelenting storms ravaging the North Sea repeatedly drove her ship back to land. The witches of Scotland and Scandinavia, James believed, had raised the storm to prevent her arrival. He had good reason to suspect they were trying to. "Ye all warne the rest of the sisters to raise the wind this day, att eleavin houris, to stay the Queen's coming in Scotland," a schoolmaster warlock named John Fian instructed three covens of about thirty-nine crones under his control.

James bravely decided to fetch his bride himself and sailed to Oslo where she had taken refuge. That royal wedding was held in the ancient Norwegian capital. Storms, attributed again to witches, impeded the King's subsequent voyage back to Scotland with his bride, but eventually the royal pair reached their bleak Caledonian realm. When she finally set foot ashore, Anne arrived not to her wedding in her new country but to her coronation. James's brooding on the power and malignancy of evil led him to write his book *Demonologi* and also to the burning of several old Danish and Scots women suspected of witchcraft.

Henrietta Maria, the French bride of Charles I, was another royal bride who gave her husband a surprise when the ship carrying her docked at Dover in 1625. The King was shocked to find her diminutive in stature and still a child physically and emotionally, though vivacious, resolute, and agile, her expressive black eyes and brown hair giving promise of the elegant beauty she would turn into. On meeting him the Princess knelt, kissed the hand of her husband-to-be, and began a set speech but burst into tears halfway through when she forgot her lines. Following this Charles and Henrietta Maria (he decided she was to be called Queen Mary) had an elaborate picnic on nearby Barham Down and then were quietly married in a ceremony not in the capital but at ancient Canterbury Cathedral. They arrived in London by royal barge, past crowds lining the banks of the Thames to Whitehall, where a great wedding banquet took place. The marriage got off to a bad start. The Queen's arrogant French entourage (she had a bishop and twenty-eight priests in tow) and her disdain for her husband's faith — Queen Mary refused to attend the Anglican rite coronation — caused great friction. Not until the King finally took action and, to the Queen's great distress, dismissed all her servants, who he realized were turning her against him, except six, did the situation rectify itself. By the third year of their marriage the couple were deeply in love. An arranged match, badly begun, turned into the happiest of marriages.

James II, another forerunner of Elizabeth and Philip, was a king whose 1678 wedding cost him his throne. When his brother Charles II, father of thirteen acknowledged illegitimate children, failed to have a child by his wife, Catherine of Braganza, he told James, then Duke of York, he must marry again. James was a widower with two daughters by his first wife but no son. The bride selected for him was the Catholic Princess Maria Beatrice d'Este, known to history as Mary of Modena, a tall, white-skinned, black-haired Italian beauty who wished to be a nun, not a wife. Like his father, Charles I, James met the bride, once the Pope had convinced her that marriage was her real vocation, at Dover. There the ratification of the proxy marriage in Modena took place, one of the most low-key weddings in the Crown's history. The reason was that Parliament had tried to prevent James from making a Catholic marriage. Though the newlywed couple made their entry to London by water like James's parents had, the marriage celebrations were subdued, consisting mainly of appearances at concerts and court balls and official visits to places like Cambridge. The long-desired son of the marriage arrived on June 10, 1688, and led to James's overthrow. By then he was King and openly acknowledged his Catholicism, and the arrival of his son, created Prince of Wales at birth, assured a Catholic succession. The Whig oligarchy raised a major no-popery scare, alleging that liberty was endangered and that the child was not the Queen's but had been smuggled into her bed in a warming pan at her lying-in. The Whig nobles invited the Dutch Prince William of Orange to come to Britain as the Protestant champion, James panicked, and the so-called Glorious

Clockwise from top left: Royal brides faced varied destinies. Eleanor of Castile's marriage with Edward I was an arranged one but her husband fell lastingly in love with her; witches called up storms to prevent Princess Anne of Denmark from crossing the sea to marry King James I; Mary of Modena's reluctant espousal of James II lost him his crown; and Henrietta Maria and Charles I's idyllic married life was the prelude to a tragic downfall.

Revolution took place, with his daughter Mary and her husband, William, usurping his throne.

Royal weddings occasionally caused their principals to act out of character. Queen Victoria, great-great-grandmother of Elizabeth II and Philip, gave her name to the Victorian era, in which the traditional role of women was emphasized. Yet because Victoria was Sovereign when she decided to marry, she, not her prospective husband, Prince Albert, had to do the proposing in October 1839, a most un-Victorian procedure. Their match was arranged but Victoria was able to choose between the two Saxe-Coburg brothers, Princes Ernest and Albert, and fast became enamoured of Albert, the younger. People's preference for romance in royal marriages should not hide the fact that arranged matches often worked out. King Edward I's marriage to Eleanor of Castile, a beautiful Spanish princess, in 1254 was negotiated by his father but turned out to be one of history's great love matches. Their wedding took place at the Monastery of Las Huelgas near Burgos, and Eleanor was a devoted wife who even accompanied her husband on crusade to the Holy Land. When she died, Edward's overwhelming grief led to the erection of the twelve huge Eleanor crosses along the route taken by her funeral cortege on its way to London.

Sometimes one royal marriage ended in another. George VI found courage to propose again to Lady Elizabeth Bowes-Lyon (who had previously turned him down) after she successfully took part as bridesmaid in his sister's wedding and seemed as a result to shed her fear of entering the Royal Family. King Michael of Romania met his future wife at Elizabeth and Philip's wedding, and Juan Carlos of Spain met his Queen-to-be at Princess Alexandra's.

As Parliament gained control of the realm's finances, obtaining a settlement to pay off debts or to maintain a married establishment became essential for a prince or princess bent on matrimony. It was the main inducement for the wedding that could be claimed as the strangest ever of an heir to the Throne. Having his considerable debts paid was the only reason the Prince of Wales, later King George IV, agreed in 1795 to marry. George, a fastidious extrovert of charm, taste, and knowledge of the arts but with a weak character, regularly fell in and out of love. Ten years before he had gone through a form of marriage with a Catholic widow, Maria Fitzherbert, that contravened the Royal Marriages Act. In 1772, after he discovered that his younger brother the Duke of Cumberland had made a secret marriage to a disreputable widow named Lady Anne Horton, the Prince of Wales's father, King George III, had talked the Government and Parliament into passing legislation called the Royal Marriages Act. The Act's object was to prevent similar misalliances among the descendants of King George II and it is still in force today. But by 1795 the Prince of Wales was comfortably under the thumb of an imperious mistress, Lady Jersey, and felt no inclination towards marriage. Once he reluctantly agreed to marry, the search for a bride was narrowed to a first cousin, Princess Caroline of Brunswick. Sir James Harris, Earl of Malmesbury, travelled to Brunswick to make the formal offer of marriage for the Prince. He found Princess Caroline intelligent, not unattractive in face, with good eyes, fine hands, and abundant hair, but also with a head too big for her body and a dumpy neck. Worse still, though good-humoured, the Princess had had a bad upbringing and was passionate, unstable, and indiscreet, and was rumoured to have a loose character. To top it all, she did not wash frequently.

Malmesbury reported none of her shortcomings or his personal view that she was unsuitable as a wife for the Heir to the Throne. After a hazardous journey through war-ravaged Europe, Caroline arrived at Greenwich to find no one on hand to meet her. When the Prince's emissary did appear, it was none other than Lady Jersey, whom Caroline knew to be his mistress. To show her power Lady Jersey insisted Caroline change her dress and

delayed the party's departure by a wrangle over seating in the carriage. Eventually Caroline made a quiet arrival at St. James's Palace. If there is love at first sight, there is also its opposite. When the Prince of Wales and Caroline came face to face, he prevented her from kneeling to him and embraced her. Proximity had a repelling effect. His Royal Highness retired to a corner of the room and said to Malmesbury, "Harris, I am not well. Pray get me a glass of brandy." Caroline's reaction was nearly as unenthusiastic. Did he always behave that way, she asked, adding, "I think he's very fat and he's nothing like as handsome as his portrait."

Marriage of the most ill-sorted bride and groom in royal history, Prince George, Prince of Wales, and Princess Caroline of Brunswick. The ceremony took place at night in 1795 and was a court event not a public one.

It was an ominous beginning. The wedding ceremony took place in the Chapel Royal, all hung with paper, giving the effect of crimson velvet, in the presence of the King, Queen, Royal Family, and Court, in the evening of April 8, 1795. The weight of the bride's dress was so great that she nearly fell over. With characteristic lack of decorum Princess Caroline talked away to her brother-in-law-to-be, the Duke of Clarence, at the altar while waiting for the Prince. When the Prince entered it was obvious that he had been drinking, for he was nervous and agitated. His manner, said Lord Melbourne, "was like a man going to execution." Finally he wept. When he and the new Princess of Wales, now officially married, withdrew to their apartments, he passed out drunk. His wife left him where he fell till he revived in the morning and slipped into her bed.

This ill-matched couple managed to remain together long enough for a daughter to be born to them, Her Royal Highness the Princess Charlotte of Wales, second in line to the Throne. But the Prince's dislike of his wife's silliness, petulance, and impropriety turned into implacable hatred expressed in persecution and meanness. The couple lived apart, Caroline in a residence near Blackheath. Her manner of life led to rumours that she had given birth to an illegitimate child, and a committee of the Privy Council conducted a "delicate investigation." Cleared of the charge but censured for her loose, unsuitable way of living, Caroline insisted she had committed adultery once only: with the husband of Maria Fitzherbert, meaning of course the Prince of Wales.

In 1811 the Prince of Wales became Regent for his incapacitated father and completely excluded his wife from court, and she left to travel abroad in 1814. Caroline was next charged with "adulterous intercourse" with her Italian courier, Bartolomeo Pergami. On her husband's succession to the Throne in 1820 the new King caused a bill of divorce to be introduced into Parliament but it died for lack of support after barely passing the House of Lords. All this time her husband's unpopularity made Caroline soar in popular esteem. Even so the King barred his despised wife from his Coronation and she died nearly three weeks later.

Had their busy lives left them time, Elizabeth and Philip could have laughed over the strange saga of royal marriages to which they had now added their own more sane and promising chapter. When royal families such as the one Elizabeth and Philip produced, but particularly those of monarchs like Edward III, George III, and Victoria with more numerous children, grow up, a spate of royal marriages usually ensues. Early in the nineteenth century a series of princely nuptials derisively termed the "royal marriage stakes" occurred from the reverse situation. The crisis was sparked by the unexpected death of Princess Charlotte of Wales. Princess Charlotte, the only child of George and Caroline's ill-fated match, was a charming girl whom her grandfather George III was set upon rescuing from the unsavoury atmosphere of Carlton House, centre of the Prince of Wales's set. It took some doing but he managed it. Amidst the growing unpopularity of George III's sons, hope centred on Charlotte. The groom chosen for her was Prince Leopold of Coburg, a clever, unaffected man of the world, though poor, who fought with the Allies in the struggle against Napoleon and later was first King of the Belgians. From his arrival at Dover on February

20, 1816, the public enthusiastically welcomed Leopold.

The wedding of Charlotte and Leopold was held not in church but at Carlton House, an altar being put up for the event in the central salon. The bride's wedding dress was said to cost over £10,000. It was a creation of transparent silver embroidered with silver lamé and worn over a white and silver slip; the trimmings were of Belgian lace and the train over thirty feet in length. Everyone noticed the clarity with which the twenty-year-old Princess made her wedding vows and how she laughed audibly when Leopold said, "with all my worldly goods I thee endow." The honeymoon was spent at Oatlands, the Duke of York's country house. All this happiness unfortunately ended in tragedy when on November 5, 1817, Princess Charlotte gave birth to a stillborn boy and died herself.

The Royal Family recognized that the Crown was at the point of crisis from the paucity of heirs. The Prince Regent had no other children; the Duke of York who was next in line was married but childless; the Duke of Clarence had a mistress, Mrs. Jordan, who had borne him ten bastards (someone quipped that he and Mrs. Jordan lived together so long that they made adultery respectable); and the fourth brother, Prince Edward, Duke of Kent, also long established with his mistress,

Princess Charlotte of Wales's wedding to Prince Leopold led to the first mass-produced souvenirs of such an event.

the charming and discreet Julie de St. Laurent, was unmarried. So was the Duke of Cambridge, and although another brother, the Duke of Cumberland, had married he was childless at the time. Three of George III's daughters were single as well.

"The country will now look to me to give them an heir to the Crown," the Duke of Kent smugly told the diarist Creevey. The hunt for brides was on. First

Cartoon satirizing the "Royal Marriage Stakes" that followed Princess Charlotte's death in 1817 leaving a dearth of heirs to the Crown.

Clarence and Kent separated themselves from their mistresses. Leopold, sorrowing widower of Princess Charlotte, pointed Kent to a sister of his, Princess Victoria of Leiningen, a well-formed, black-eyed, brunette beauty who had just lost her husband. Once assured that Parliament would provide him with a new settlement, Kent was soon in the state drawing room of Schloss Ehrenburg being joined in marriage to the Princess, who wore orange blossoms and white roses on her silk dress for the service. Clarence selected Princess Adelaide of Saxe-Meiningen as his wife-to-be. The brothers and their brides, one in gold and the other in silver, were then married jointly in an afternoon ceremony at the Queen's House in Kew on July 11, 1818. Clarence won the royal marriage stakes in that he produced the first child, a daughter who died, soon followed by a second who lived just a year, but it was Kent's only child, Alexandrina Victoria, who inherited the Crown as Queen Victoria.

Wedding of Queen Victoria and Prince Albert at the Chapel Royal, St. James's Palace. The ceremony was modelled on that of Victoria's grandparents, King George III and Queen Charlotte.

The most marked change in royal weddings after the Georgian age, and which reached its zenith in the married life of Elizabeth and Philip, was the increasing involvement of the public in them. This development mirrored the greater participation of the subject in the whole process of governing, through the growth of newspapers and the mass media, the reforming of Parliament, and the extending of the franchise. At their wedding in 1795 George and Caroline did not bother to show themselves to the public. The ordinary person was always keen to see a new princess or prince but the ritual showing of them was to the constitutional and social elite. From the time of Princess Charlotte's wedding in 1816, the process that would lead to a billion viewers watching the wedding of Prince Charles, the Prince of Wales, and Lady Diana Spencer was underway. One symbol of the trend was the sudden importance and popularity of mass-produced commemorative souvenirs of royal weddings.

The pattern for Victorian Royal Family espousals was established by Queen Victoria's own wedding in 1840, which was itself modelled on that of her grandparents, King George III and Queen Charlotte. Victoria's marriage was the quintessential romantic love match. Victoria vetoed heavy royal robes for the ceremony in favour of court dress, simple but with a six-yard train and lace that took more than two hundred people nine months to make, though at the last minute the Queen reduced the length of her train. The dresses of her bridesmaids she designed herself. The Chapel Royal at St. James's Palace was chosen for the short exchange of vows on February 10, 1840. Few royal brides have recorded their wedding days but Victoria was one who did: "I wore a white satin gown with a very deep flounce of Honiton lace. I wore my Turkish diamond necklace and earrings, and Albert's beautiful sapphire brooch," she wrote, adding, "They cheered us really most warmly and heartily; the crowd was immense; and the Hall at Buckingham Palace was full of people; they cheered us again and again." Victoria's is the last wedding of a reigning monarch. All her successors since 1840 have married before inheriting the Crown.

Queen Victoria and Prince Albert arranged marriages for their children but agreed they would never force them to wed if unwilling. The Queen hated to part with her children, so in the end she allowed them to marry non-royal spouses at home. Her fourth daughter Princess Louise's marriage to the Marquis of Lorne established this precedent.

By doing this, the Queen was easing the transition to the age when a royal marriage would be entirely the choice of the prince or princess in question. Her husband Albert's demise in 1861 affected royal marriages too. Victoria's daughter Alice had been engaged to the Grand Duke of Hesse since 1860, but because of her father's death her wedding had to be postponed until 1862. Even then it was a small affair, held in the dining room at Osborne House with few guests, the men in black and the ladies in grey, the Queen herself in sombre mourning.

Victoria's determination to remain in widowed seclusion caused her to decree that the important marriage of Prince Albert Edward, the Prince of Wales, future King Edward VII, on March 10, 1863, be held in St. George's Chapel, Windsor. The last member of the Royal Family to marry there had been Edward the Black Prince in 1361. The bride of the Prince of Wales was the ethereally lovely Alexandra of Denmark, whom he met in an arranged "accidental" encounter. No witches strove to prevent the arrival of this "Sea Kings' daughter from over the sea, Alexandra!" as Tennyson hailed her; far from it, the public fell in love with her the moment she stepped ashore at Gravesend and continued to adore her until her death in 1925. Magnificent as their wedding was — the bride in court dress of white satin, Jenny Lind's glorious voice raised in a hymn composed by the Prince Consort, the Knights of the Garter present in their blue mantles — mourning had been decreed for it and Queen Victoria was not visible, having chosen a vantage point above the choir where, head crowned with black widow's cap, she could see but not be seen. Public disappointment was voiced.

A grieving Queen Victoria watched the marriage of her eldest son the Prince of Wales (King Edward VII) from a special box from which she could see but not be seen.

Except for Princess Beatrice and Prince Alfred, Duke of Edinburgh, Victoria's other children were also married at Windsor. Beatrice chose the small parish church of St. Mildred near Osborne in the Isle of Wight for her wedding to Prince Henry of Battenberg on July 23, 1885. This marriage provoked a temporary breach between mother and daughter, for Queen Victoria had expected her youngest child would not wed. Victorian royal brides invariably wore dresses decorated with orange blossoms that were avidly described in contemporary newspapers and magazines, while Victorian royal grooms kept to the practice of wearing uniform. For his marriage to the Grand Duchess Marie, Prince Alfred, Duke of Edinburgh, a career naval officer, donned the uniform of the Imperial Russian Navy to compliment his bride. Victorian nuptial entertainments were first, followed by wedding breakfasts at Buckingham Palace, later at Windsor, and receptions in the Waterloo Gallery.

The 1893 wedding of Victoria's grandson Prince George of Wales to Princess May of Teck sensibly shifted the matrimonial scene back to London. Princess Maud of Wales therefore was wed at Buckingham Palace on July 22, 1896, to Prince Charles of Denmark, soon to become King Haakon VII of Norway. The athletic Maud continued another recent innovation: asking relatives to be bridesmaids. Queen Victoria was present, and the colours selected for the dresses were red and white, the royal colours of Denmark.

The increasing importance of the Commonwealth was evident in the first major royal wedding after the First World War, that of Princess Mary, later the Princess Royal, to Viscount Lascelles, later Earl of Harewood, in 1922. The bride's white silk train

One royal wedding often led to another. Lady Elizabeth Bowes-Lyon was bridesmaid at Princess Mary's wedding on February 28, 1922, to Viscount Lascelles. Participation in this royal ceremony gave her confidence to reconsider marrying the Duke of York, whose proposal she had turned down the previous year. Engraving of the Frank Salisbury painting.

included maple leaves for Canada and ferns for New Zealand, with lotuses of India on the border, as well as roses, thistles, shamrocks, and daffodils. On the wedding cake were the symbols of the Girl Guides, whose president she was, and of her regiment. The wedding of Elizabeth II's parents, the Duke of York and Lady Elizabeth Bowes-Lyon, marked another step in the development of royal wedding practice, for it was the first to be filmed. The man and woman in the street were able to see it at the cinema the evening of the wedding day, April 26, 1923. In 1934 the Kents' wedding was broadcast by radio.

Royal weddings of Queen Elizabeth II's reign continued the trends already noticed and reflected rapid changes in society. As the only sister of the Sovereign, Princess Margaret had a major wedding, being given away by the Duke of Edinburgh. The streets of London were decorated, and the ceremony in Westminster Abbey on May 6, 1960, exhibited the influence of her talented and artistic photographer husband, Anthony Armstrong-Jones, created Earl of Snowdon the next year. Margaret's wedding dress, relying on line, was a study in simplicity, the upper part consisting of light transparent silk. The Queen's daughter, Princess Anne, was chief bridesmaid. Building on the experience of the Coronation, the service was broadcast live, the first royal wedding to be televised. With the marriage of Princess Patricia of Connaught in 1919, Westminster Abbey had become the favoured venue for royal nuptials, but when the Duke of Kent married a pretty blond named Miss Katharine Worsley in 1962, historic York Minster was chosen for the ceremony, the

Commemorative souvenir booklet of the wedding of Princess Margaret and Anthony Armstrong-Jones (later Earl of Snowdon) in 1960. Prince Philip gave the bride away.

bride's family being Yorkshire baronets. Like the Princess of Wales's would be in 1981, Katharine's dress was designed with the wedding setting in mind. It was of white silk French gauze in layers of organdie and ended in a fifteen-foot train flowing from the waist. The reception was on the lawn of Hovingham Hall, the family seat, and with the great marquees and two thousand guests seemed like a huge garden party.

A lovely royal bride of 1962, Katharine Worsley, Duchess of Kent.

The Queen's popular cousin Princess Alexandra weds the Hon. (later Sir) Angus Ogilvy.

Princess Anne's mediaeval-style dress was a distinctive feature of her wedding in 1973 to Captain Mark Phillips.

The entire world was caught up in the fairy-tale but ill-fated wedding of the Prince of Wales to Lady Diana Spencer.

Princess Anne, later Princess Royal, was chief bridesmaid at Princess Margaret's wedding and at those of her cousins the Duke of Kent and Princess Alexandra. Her own turn came in 1973 when she married Captain Mark Phillips. The technical advance marking this royal wedding was the televising of the Abbey ceremony in colour. The Princess's dress of soft white satin had a high neckline, tailored bodice, a short train, and sleeves that gave it a striking mediaeval look. The groom wore the uniform of his regiment the Queen's Bays and used his sword to cut the wedding cake.

In view of subsequent events, the memory of the wedding of the Prince of Wales to the beautiful young Lady Diana Spencer on July 29, 1981, has a bittersweet quality but undoubtedly it was the royal wedding par excellence of the twentieth century. St. Paul's Cathedral was chosen for the ceremony on account of its seating capacity and because of the architecturally minded Prince of Wales's affection

for it as an historic building. Nigel Arch and Joanna Marschner, in their book *The Royal Wedding Dresses*, quote the designers of Diana's ivory silk taffeta wedding dress, with its spectacular twenty-foot train, as saying their aim was to transform the bride into a romantic fairy-tale princess. They did so with great success. On the day of the wedding the whole world seemed to stop to watch this electrifying extravaganza. It seemed the epitome of the triumph of love. Dress for the pages taking part was suitably naval uniform of 1863, the date of the last marriage of a Prince of Wales. The bride and groom imitated Elizabeth and Philip by spending the first few days of their honeymoon at Broadlands, sleeping in the very bed used in 1947. The Monarchy looked as though it had rejuvenated itself once again. Few suspected that the media was now controlling, not just reporting, set on turning the new Princess of Wales into a fashion model and superstar, two roles at variance with the royal one.

(Above) Elizabeth and Philip's second son, Prince Andrew, Duke of York, leaves Westminster Abbey with his bride, Miss Sarah Ferguson.

(Left) Exchange of vows between the Queen and Duke's youngest son, Prince Edward, Earl of Wessex, and Miss Sophie Rhys-Jones at St. George's Chapel, Windsor.

Queen Victoria established many royal wedding traditions, including the off-the-face bridal veil and bridal bouquet with myrtle, both seen in the wedding picture of Queen Mary's niece Lady May Cambridge (left); and the custom of the bride and groom showing themselves to the public on the Buckingham Palace balcony, as seen in this photo of Prince Andrew, Duke of York, and Miss Sarah Ferguson (above).

The 1981 wedding set the pattern for the rest of the century. The Duke of York's marriage in 1986 was a rerun on a smaller scale. After the marital breakups and other misfortunes of the 1990s, the wedding of Prince Edward and Sophie Rhys-Jones in 1999 was a more modest affair, significantly being held at Windsor, planned by a groom skilled in dealing with the media. Nonetheless, the twentieth century had consolidated royal wedding traditions.

A number of practices begun by Queen Victoria, including the bride wearing an off-the-face veil to allow her to be seen, the recourse to relatives for bridesmaids, and the appearance of the bride and groom on the balcony of Buckingham Palace so that the people might see them — a custom Victoria began with the wedding of her eldest daughter the Princess Royal in 1858 — remain regular features of royal weddings. Royal brides continue to carry myrtle grown from a plant descended from Queen Victoria's own wedding bouquet, royal wedding rings are still made from Welsh gold, the bride's dress has a court train and, the groom is almost always wed in uniform. And the Queen declares her consent to family marriages to her Privy Council for Canada as routinely as she does to her United Kingdom one.

These usages blend with new faces, a different type of bride or groom, kisses in public, a society diverse in culture and creed, and the importance of television in design of bridal attire. Royal weddings remain important affairs of state. They are the focus of loyalty to the Queen, her husband, and her family; they evoke interest and pride in the splendour and continuity of the Crown. The vast increase in public participation in them, even those that have foundered, far from diminishing their special nature or detracting from the appeal of Elizabeth and Philip's family, has enhanced their popularity.

Consorts

There have been eight consorts to queens regnant in our British and Commonwealth history: Philip of Spain (Mary I), William of Orange (Mary II), George of Denmark (Anne), Albert of Saxe-Coburg-Gotha (Victoria), and Philip of Greece (Elizabeth II) in the English line. A sixth English Queen, Elizabeth I, did not marry. Mary Queen of Scots had three consorts — Francis II of France, Henry Stuart (Lord Darnley), and James Hepburn (Earl of Bothwell), the latter two Scots.

One of the common challenges facing a male consort was obvious to Prince Philip, Duke of Edinburgh, who said of the Queen, "Because she is the Sovereign everyone turns to her. If you have a King and Queen, there are certain things people automatically go to the Queen about. But if the Queen is also the *Queen*, they go to her about everything." And Prince Albert, the Prince Consort,

observed, "A very considerable section of the nation had never given itself the trouble to consider what really is the position of the husband of a Queen Regnant. When I first came over here, I was met by this want of knowledge and unwillingness to give a thought to the position of this luckless personage."

Male consorts, unlike their female counterparts, have, as consorts, no right to be crowned or anointed and they remain in law subjects of their Queen. Because there is no written, or even customary, constitutional status or role for the consort, each had vastly different experiences, while sharing some common trials.

It is often said that when one weds one marries not only a spouse but also his or her family, sometimes with wonderful benefits and sometimes with dire consequences. For royal marriages the personal travails are overwhelmed by the even greater political consequences. In the musical *Camelot* the wise King Arthur remarks ruefully that the old adage "blood is thicker than water" was promulgated by "undeserving relatives." In the more deadly real world of the Wars of the Roses and the intrigues of King Henry VIII's many in-laws from his multiple wives, England's royal family quarrels made the land run red with blood. To some it seemed far better for kings to marry foreign princesses, whose relatives for the most part stayed beyond the silver sea that served Shakespeare's sceptred isle as a moat, than Englishwomen, whose brothers, uncles, and cousins were either noblemen seeking to expand their power or gentry seeking to be ennobled, with jealous rivals ready to become enemies of the king if they were. But to others in England all foreigners were suspect at best and anathema at worst. Since the ideal consort, one who was neither British nor a foreigner, could not exist, each monarch had to decide which way to look. Each queen, except for Elizabeth I, who chose no consort, chose an outsider, though Mary, Queen of Scots

Queen Mary I was the first Queen Regnant.

tried both, marrying a foreigner and two Scots.

The dilemmas facing queens were greater than those facing kings. Although in theory both England and Scotland, not having the Salic law, recognized a woman's right to the Throne, it was not until King Henry VIII's daughter Mary I became Queen that a woman successfully held her claim to the Throne in England. And Mary, Queen of Scots was the first real Scottish Queen Regnant at the same time. In England it was understood that a woman shared in her husband's dignity by common law but a husband had no such claim on his wife's dignity. However, it was also true that a woman's possessions generally belonged to her husband. How did these principles apply to a queen and her consort? Was a powerful husband an asset to the kingdom or a threat to its independence? There was no universally accepted answer.

The modern world, if it remembers the Spanish Armada at all, remembers the gallant Sir Francis Drake playing bowls before despatching the Spanish galleons with the aid of a favourable wind, saving England from conquest. It may also remember the religious conflicts between Catholics and Protestants that underpinned the war and the geopolitical rivalry between a venerable Continental power and an upstart seafaring island. But it has generally been forgotten that the Spanish King who ordered the unsuccessful Armada to sea in 1588 had once been King of England.

When Mary I became the first Queen Regnant of England the question of the rights of her husband

and consort became of paramount constitutional and geopolitical significance. In 1518, at the age of two, she was betrothed to the six-month-old Francis, Dauphin of France. The betrothal, a political arrangement by her father, King Henry VIII, was allowed to lapse, and at the age of six she was betrothed a second time, to the Holy Roman Emperor Charles V. This betrothal too was allowed to lapse. King Henry, who at the time did not have a son to inherit the Throne, worried that Mary would succeed him — a prospect that raised the concern that her future husband would absorb England into his own domains. So Henry leaned first to the French, then to the Spanish, and also considered the Scottish, but in the end he didn't wish to commit to any foreign alliance for his daughter.

When Mary eventually succeeded her half-brother, Edward VI, as monarch, the question of a consort was for her to decide. She chose the Habsburg Prince Philip of Spain, son and heir to Charles V, Holy Roman Emperor and King of Spain and its empire in the Americas, the Netherlands, and several other domains and her former betrothed. Prince Philip was co-regent, with his grandmother, for Spain, as the Emperor spent most of his time in Brussels. It was the Emperor, himself a cousin of Queen Mary, who arranged the marriage. Needing an English alliance for his wars with France the Emperor briefly considered renewing his own suit as a widower for the now thirty-seven-year-old spinster but opted instead to advance his twenty-seven-year-old son as the suitable candidate.

The marriage was strictly a political arrangement. The betrothed had never met and only exchanged portraits. For Mary it was her duty as Queen

Philip II of Spain, husband of Queen Mary I, was the first Consort to a Queen Regnant. His experience highlighted the challenges his successors faced.

to marry and produce an heir. She remarked to the Emperor's ambassador Simon Renard that "she had never felt that which was called love, nor harboured thoughts of voluptuousness, and had never considered marriage until God had been pleased to raise her to the Throne." For Philip the marriage was a duty to his father and emperor.

Although the Queen was marrying on the advice of her Council, the Council was in fact split between the pro-Spanish and pro-French factions and those against any foreign Catholic marriage. These passions were aflame in the country as a whole.

The proclamation of the wedding precipitated a rebellion in the more Protestant south of England. In the southwest and midlands it was put down quickly, but in the southeast Sir Thomas Wyatt led some seven thousand men on London. This threat too was successfully stopped but the fear it engendered led to the execution of Lady Jane Grey, a Protestant great-niece of Henry VIII and claimant to the Throne. It was a bad start to the marriage.

The Emperor smoothed the way for Philip's entry to England through financial rewards and bribes. One of his emissaries, the Count of Egmont, cynically said of Tudor England, "More is to be done with money here than in any other country in the world." To raise his son to Mary's equal the Emperor also presented him with the Kingdom of Naples, which he would not otherwise inherit until his father's death, thus making him a king and not merely a prince on the day of his wedding.

The Royal Marriages Bill, which finally passed Parliament on April 12, 1554, provided that Philip and Mary would share equally their titles and honours, the senior being King and Queen of England. Philip would share in the government, but all of England's rights, privileges, and customs would remain, its sovereignty was vested in the Queen, and no foreigner could hold office. English would be the language of business and England was not to be involved in wars between the Empire and France. If there were children the succession would be according to English law but if there was no issue and Mary died before Philip the King would have no right of his own to the Throne and his status would cease.

After the wedding the couple were proclaimed "King and Queen Philip and Mary, by the Grace of God King and Queen of England, France, Naples, Jerusalem, Ireland, Defenders of the Faith and Princes of Spain and Sicily, Archdukes of Austria, Dukes of Milan, Burgundy and Brabant, Counts of Habsburg, Flanders and Tyrol." Philip's name appeared in all laws passed in England, but he was furious that he was not crowned as King.

Philip remained in England for a year and in September 1555 he left for Brussels. In that year he proved himself to be a devoted and considerate husband and a tactful and intelligent monarch who won over the Court and Council with his adaptation to English ways and his scrupulous observance of the marriage agreement. He was even named regent for the prospective child when it was thought, incorrectly as it turned out, that Mary was pregnant. He helped his wife restore Catholic rights in England, which was seen as good or bad, depending upon the commentator's bias, but he was more tolerant than his supporters or opponents. While English history has been unkind to him because of the later history of the Armada, he was actually quite popular and successful in the eyes of his English people at the time. He left for Brussels to attend to Imperial concerns, and in January 1556 the Emperor abdicated the rest of Philip's inheritance to him. Philip and Mary were now the King and Queen of Spain and its empire. A truce with France meant that Philip did not need English assistance, and he remained absent for a year and a half. Then in 1557 his relations with the Pope soured, leading to war in Italy. The French sided with the Pope and Philip returned to England to seek military aid. Because the French had been intriguing in English affairs as well, the English saw themselves not being drawn into a Spanish quarrel but serving their own interests by supporting Philip's war. But their involvement led to the loss of Calais, the last remnant of England's Norman lands on the Continent. Philip left England again in August for the battles in the Low Countries. However, in November Queen Mary died and Philip ceased to be King of England.

With the death of his English wife, Philip II hinted that he might seek the hand of her half-sister and successor Queen Elizabeth I, as he wished to keep the ties that he had developed with England. Elizabeth considered but rejected the offer. The friendship between the two realms deteriorated, and by 1587 they were at war and the Armada was being readied to sail into history. Philip's experience as the first consort to a queen demonstrated all the dangers, frustrations, challenges, and opportunities to be faced by his successors in their turn.

Having seen off the former husband of her late half-sister, Queen Elizabeth I was in no hurry to alienate her people by acquiring a foreign husband of her own and was fully aware of her father's problems in acquiring a domestic wife. The experience of her cousin Mary, Queen of Scots, whose husband, Lord Darnley, was murdered by jealous Scottish nobles, was also a warning. So, although a committed Protestant who readily persecuted her Catholic subjects, whom she mistrusted, Elizabeth borrowed heavily from the Catholic cult of the Virgin Mary. She emerged as the "Virgin Queen," showered by her admirers with many of the attributes of the celestial Queen. There were many courtiers for Elizabeth I but no consort.

In Scotland, the situation had been quite similar to this point in history, with only two examples to consider. In 1286, when she was three years old,

and just after her accession to the Scottish Throne, Queen Margaret was engaged to Prince Edward, son of King Edward I of England and future King Edward II. Margaret was the granddaughter of King Alexander III and daughter of Princess Margaret and King Erik II of Norway. Although she died en route to England from Norway at the age of seven and never married Edward, the terms of the arranged marriage agreement emphasized the concerns of political marriages and the roles of

Francis II of France had a short-lived, politically arranged marriage to Mary, Queen of Scots.

consorts. The English King Edward I's motive was clearly to attempt to unite Scotland to England. The regents of Scotland insisted on provisions in the marriage contract that the "rights, laws, liberties and customs of Scotland" were to be "wholly and inviolably preserved" and that Scotland was to remain "separate and divided from the Kingdom of England." King Edward I agreed because he was confident that his son would eventually ignore the terms and unite the two kingdoms in fact if not in name.

The consorts of Mary, Queen of Scots highlighted the political nature of international marriages and the dangerous nature of domestic ones. As a child Mary became Queen Regnant of Scotland and she was also the heir to her English Tudor cousins, Edward VI, Mary I, and Elizabeth I. Henry VIII tried to arrange a marriage between her and Edward but it came to naught as the Scots rightly understood that Henry saw it as a means once again to merge England and Scotland. Instead she was married in 1558 to Prince Francis, son of King Henry II of France. When he became King Francis II he was King of France, consort to the Queen of Scotland, and consort to the heir to the childless and unmarried Queen of England and Ireland.

Lord Darnley, Mary, Queen of Scots' second husband, was murdered by Scottish lords, but he is the ancestor of today's Royal Family and those of many countries.

The Earl of Bothwell, implicated in the murder of Lord Darnley, was forced into exile after he married Queen Mary.

The potential of uniting the four kingdoms was very real. But when Francis II died before he and Mary could have a child, the French succession passed to his brother and Mary returned to Scotland as a widow and Queen. In Scotland in 1565 she married her cousin Henry Stuart, Lord Darnley, but his irresponsible and arrogant behaviour earned the enmity of other Scottish lords and he was murdered less than two years later, possibly with the approval of Queen Mary. Three months later she married James Hepburn, Earl of Bothwell, who was believed by many Scots to be behind Darnley's murder. More Scottish lords rose in outrage, Bothwell was forced into exile, and Mary was compelled to abdicate in favour of her son by Lord Darnley, King James VI. Mary was eventually arrested and ultimately executed, in 1587, by her cousin Elizabeth I, and upon the latter's death, Mary's son James succeeded to the English Throne as James I, though in her will Mary had disinherited her son as King of England in favour of King Philip II of Spain, another basis for the former English King's unsuccessful attempt to conquer England through the Armada. Through King James I and VI the English and Scottish thrones were united in one monarch and eventually the two kingdoms themselves were united into Great Britain.

Having made it clear with Philip II that foreign male consorts were to have no claim to the Crown of England, the British Parliament took the opposite position with William of Orange. The difference of course was that Philip was a Catholic they did not wish to have while William was a Protestant they did wish to have.

William was the great anomaly of the consorts, largely because he wasn't really a consort. The Whig magnates who overthrew the Catholic King James II upon the birth of his Catholic son in 1688 did not do so to replace him with his daughter Mary: they wanted Mary's Protestant husband, William. But

William of Orange was Co-Sovereign with Queen Mary II and, as King William III, took precedence over his wife, as reflected in this engraving.

while William was in line to the Throne they could not pretend he was King by succession. He had become King by conquest. This was not unheard of in British history. King William the Conqueror, King Henry IV, and King Henry VII were junior members of the Blood Royal who acquired the Throne in that manner. In legal fiction Parliament declared that the Throne had been abandoned by James II and offered to William III and Mary II by Parliament. But the fact that Mary II was the daughter and adult Protestant heir to James provided a claim to legitimacy. Thus William and Mary were co-sovereigns, being King and Queen Regnant and King and Queen Consort at the same time.

But the co-sovereignty was also a legal fiction. The Bill of Rights, by which they took the Throne, explicitly stated that the "sole and full exercise of the royal powers be only in and executed by the said prince of Orange in the name of the said prince and princess during their joint lives." Mary reigned only when William was out of the country.

When Queen Mary II died in 1694 King William III continued as sole monarch until he died in 1702. Only in 1702 did the Crown pass to Mary's sister Anne, William and Mary having no children. William therefore faced none of the constraints of a consort, being first and foremost a monarch is his own right.

Prince George of Denmark, the consort of Queen Anne, is probably the least remembered and the least influential of all the consorts. He was apparently quite happy with both circumstances. Already married to Anne for nineteen years when she ascended the Throne in 1702, he was described by many contemporaries as a lethargic figure who was given no real power. He was nominally Generalissimo and Lord High Admiral, but the army was controlled by John Churchill, 1st Duke of Marlborough, and the

In honour of "King Billy," William III banners lead many Orange Day parades in Canada. But, as controversial monarchs, William and Mary were reviled by Jacobites as "The Orange and The Lemon."

Admiralty by the latter's brother, Admiral George Churchill. The Prince was criticized for cronyism in his appointments at the Admiralty and indifference to the corruption that existed in the department.

Queen Anne wished to make George the King Consort but was prevented from doing so, though she appointed him to the Order of the Garter and he led the homage at her Coronation. He had been made Duke of Cumberland in the reign of William and Mary and thus sat in the House of Lords. This caused some difficulties when, as the Queen's Consort, he had to abstain in some votes and vote against his own interests on such issues as the Occasional Conformity Bill, which would have prevented non-Anglicans from avoiding the Test Act (requiring office holders to be Anglicans) by occasional attendance at Anglican services and then regular attendance at their own. Prince George himself was a Lutheran with his own private chapel and took the Anglican sacrament once a year.

In his private life he was regarded as an attentive husband, but even his private role as consort proved tragically ineffective. All monarchs, male or female, feel the obligation to produce an heir. Queen Anne and Prince George had twelve children but all died at birth or as young children.

When Prince George died on October 28, 1708, the Queen said, "The loss of such a husband, who loved me so dearly and so devotedly, is too crushing for me to be able to bear it as I ought." And though his influence was considered minimal, it was not totally absent. Sir Winston Churchill, describing the brilliance of Queen Anne's court and its achievements, noted that Prince George was nevertheless "one of the linchpins in that

Prince George of Denmark was a dutiful husband and support to Queen Anne and is largely forgotten in history.

marvellous coach of state that drove so triumphantly along the roads of Europe." A contemporary, the Earl of Westmoreland, said, after the Prince's death, "He kept the Queen from being beguiled to her dishonour by sycophants that were about her all the time of his life."

The consort of Queen Victoria, Prince Albert, the Prince Consort, is probably the most famous of the consorts and has the greatest reputation for achievement prior to the Duke of Edinburgh. It

While not accorded the official status held by William III, Prince Albert was almost Co-Sovereign with Queen Victoria through his behind-the-scenes influence.

is one of those rare cases when the facts merit the reputation.

Prince Albert was born in 1819, the younger son of Ernst, Duke of Saxe-Coburg-Gotha. He first met Princess Victoria in 1836 and they were married on February 10, 1840, when the Queen had been on the Throne for nearly three years. After the marriage he was made a Knight of the Garter and a Privy Councillor. Victoria wished to make Albert King Consort but Lord Melbourne, the Prime Minister, objected, so he remained Prince Albert of Saxe-Coburg-Gotha until 1857, when the Queen created him Prince Consort. He had been Regent Designate since an attempt on the Queen's life early in her reign.

While he had no formal powers beyond his role as the Queen's Private Secretary, he was a power behind the Throne. He had written to Lord Melbourne, "I must alone be her adviser." He had full access to cabinet and other state papers and from 1841 attended audiences with ministers.

His greatest constitutional contribution was to "de-partisanize" the Crown. In the past, even after responsible ministerial government evolved, the Monarch openly had favourites among competing politicians. Queen Victoria had started the same way with her affection for Lord Melbourne. Prince Albert dramatically changed that. He maintained that the Crown should be non-partisan but not necessarily non-political. The Crown had the right, and the duty, to encourage policies that were best for the Empire but should not care (and he did not care) which politicians were in power to carry them out.

In foreign affairs the Prince was a great asset through his many European connections and his wise counsel, helping to avert war with the United States just before he died in 1861. In many ways he was co-sovereign with Queen Victoria in practice if not in name.

The Prince Consort's other great area of contribution was in the realm between the role

Victoria, Albert, and their family at the opening of the Great Exhibition of 1851, one of Prince Albert's major achievements.

of the state and the purely private life of a royal. The Prince was responsible for cataloguing and enhancing the Royal Collection, promoted public concerts and other amenities for people on Sundays, and was President of the Fine Arts Commission and Chancellor of Cambridge University. He founded Imperial College in London as the first university dedicated to scientific research. He generally promoted science and the arts and is perhaps best remembered in this field for staging in London the Great Exhibition of 1851, which was the forerunner of all the famous world's fairs that followed in the twentieth century from New York in 1939 to Montreal in 1967 and Vancouver in 1986.

THE QUEEN AND PRINCE ALBERT.

After his death the Prince Consort became an iconic figure to his widow Queen Victoria and in the folklore of the Empire. The Victoria and Albert statue at Windsor Castle presents a romantic image of the Prince (left). The first day cover in 1978, commemorating the one hundredth anniversary of Capex, featured reproductions of nineteenth-century stamps of Victoria and Albert issued by Canada Post (above).

In domestic life the Prince was clearly the head of the household with both positive and negative effects. He set a high standard both for his own family and for the Queen's people to follow and it was a good standard, but he never understood his eldest son, Prince Albert Edward, the Prince of Wales, which led to tension in the Royal Family and wasted opportunities for the Prince. Albert built Balmoral Castle as a fantastical and mythical Scottish castle, but the myth became a reality with time and still impresses people today. He also improved the royal household's operations and acquired the estate at Osborne and designed the new house. And last but not least he was responsible for popularizing the Christmas tree of his native Germany. The portrait of the Queen and her Consort and their children around the tree at Christmas was published not only in Britain but also in Canada, the United States, and throughout the Empire and beyond. It is unquestionably to Prince Albert that the world owes the modern religious and commercial fascination with the Christmas tree, which would otherwise likely have remained a quaint German custom not noted elsewhere, if it had even survived into the modern world.

But Prince Albert remained too reserved to be fully embraced by the people of his adopted land.

When he died of typhoid fever on December 14, 1861, it would be fair to say that he was greatly respected but not loved by the people. But as he set high standards for his family and his adopted people to live up to, he also set high standards for his successors as consorts to live up to.

Prince Philip has lost and acquired numerous titles and positions since his engagement to Princess Elizabeth. He was born Prince Philip of Schleswig-Holstein-Sonderburg-Glucksburg and a Prince of Greece and Denmark, as the grandson of the King of Greece and great-grandson of the King of Denmark. While retaining these titles, with the abolition of the Greek monarchy and his family's life in exile he adopted Mountbatten, the Anglicized form of his mother's maiden name, and became Philip Mountbatten when he joined the Royal Navy.

In 1947 Lieutenant Philip Mountbatten became a British subject and renounced his Greek titles and place in succession to the Greek throne. It was assumed at the time that this was because he was marrying Princess Elizabeth. In fact, while the marriage was the final trigger in the event, the process had begun much earlier when he decided he wished to become a long-service naval officer, which necessitated him acquiring British subject status. It was put off until after the war and then put off once again when the restored Greek monarchy was under attack by Communist insurgents. Since Prince Philip was already linked with Princess Elizabeth in public speculation, the British Government felt that if he renounced his Greek status it would be seen as British belief that the Communists were winning. By 1947 the monarchy was, for a time, secure in Greece and the engagement was announced, so the formal

Prince Philip was considered both Greek and British when he became engaged to Princess Elizabeth and his official status was diplomatically addressed.

decision for Philip to become a British subject was politically acceptable.

The irony of all the hand-wringing over Philip becoming British emerged a decade later when Prince Ernest of Hanover went to court in Britain to have his status as a British subject recognized as a descendant of the Electress Sophia. The Electress

Sophia Naturalisation Act of 1705 had made Sophia the Electress of Hanover, the next Protestant heir to Queen Anne, and all her descendants in perpetuity British subjects. She died before Queen Anne but her son became King George I. The British courts ruled in favour of Prince Ernest, confirming that the Sophia Naturalisation Act was still in effect for descendants of Sophia born before 1948, when it was revoked for the United Kingdom. Therefore it also applied to Prince Philip, another descendant of Sophia. He had in fact always been a British subject and did not need to become one in 1947, but neither the Royal Family, the British Government, nor the British people had realized it. The charade of making him "British" was a continuation of the age-old fear of foreign consorts and entanglements.

Unlike his predecessor as consort, Philip received certain titles and status quite quickly. For his wedding he was created His Royal Highness and Duke of Edinburgh by King George VI. This made him a

The Duke of Edinburgh was appointed a member of the Queen's Privy Council for Canada by Her Majesty at a Council meeting in Ottawa in 1957.

peer of the realm, a status not held by Prince Albert. In 1951 the King also made him a Privy Councillor. In September of 1952 the Queen elevated him to next in precedence to herself and at the Coronation he was the first layman to do homage to the new Queen. In 1953 he became Regent Designate for his son Prince Charles until 1966, when Charles came of age. He was also appointed a Counsellor of State, one of the designated members of the Royal Family who act on the Queen's behalf when she is out of the United Kingdom. On February 22, 1957, the Queen created the Duke a Prince of the United Kingdom, equivalent to the status he held as a Greek prince.

The Canadian Prime Minister, John Diefenbaker, also contributed to the Duke's elevation in status. As an opposition Member of Parliament Diefenbaker had advocated in 1952 that the Duke of Edinburgh be made a Prince of the Commonwealth. Nothing came of his suggestion, but in 1957, as the new Prime Minister of Canada, he advised the Queen to create the Duke a member of the Queen's Privy Council for Canada. This took place in Ottawa during the 1957 tour, and in 2007 the Prince is second in seniority among Canadian Privy Councillors. It has also been argued, but not tested in court, that the Canadian Citizenship Act makes those individuals who are British subjects under the Electress Sophia Naturalisation Act also Canadian citizens. If valid then Prince Philip automatically acquired Canadian citizenship in 1947 when Canadian citizenship was created.

One critical thing Prince Philip was not allowed to contribute to the Crown was the name of a new dynasty. Mary, Queen of Scots was the first queen regnant to leave an heir, but her husband, Lord Darnley, was also her cousin and a Stuart, so the dynastic name did not change. The next child of a male consort to become monarch, the eldest son of Queen Victoria, King Edward VII, assumed the dynastic name of his father, Prince Albert, and the reigning house changed from the House of Brunswick (sometimes called the House of Hanover) to the House of Saxe-Coburg-Gotha. In 1917, reacting to anti-German sentiment, King George V, grandson of Prince Albert, changed the name to the House of Windsor, after the royal castle.

Prince Philip apparently expected, as did his uncle Lord Mountbatten who promoted the idea, that when Prince Charles, Prince of Wales, succeeded to the Throne he would be the first of the House of Mountbatten, or perhaps Mountbatten-Windsor or Windsor-Mountbatten as a compromise. But the Queen's advisers were against the idea, and, to put an end to the speculation very early, on April 9, 1952, the Queen declared in Council that her heirs would remain the House of Windsor.

Much has been made of how this was a snub of the Duke of Edinburgh, and to some extent it is true, but there were nuances to the circumstances that must also be acknowledged. Windsor is not really a dynastic name as were those of the past. If not for the Great War the Queen would be a monarch of the House of Saxe-Coburg-Gotha. Windsor was adopted because it was a generic name associated with the Crown itself and not a house name identified with a specific royal branch. Any of the dynasties — Norman, Plantagenet, Tudor, Stuart, or Brunswick — not just the House of Saxe-Coburg-Gotha, could also have claimed to be called the House of Windsor. Although it was not specifically stated it was probably thought in

Coronation photographic portrait of the Queen and her Consort, the Duke of Edinburgh. Unlike Prince Albert, the Duke would not give his name to a new dynasty.

1917, and the attitude grew, that the name of the Royal House would not need to change again, and Windsor would remain regardless of the consort. So the Queen's decision was not a reflection on Prince Philip personally.

At the same time Mountbatten is not the dynastic name of the Duke of Edinburgh in any event. It is the anglicized form of his mother's maiden name of Battenberg, changed in 1917 for the same reason the King made his change. The Duke's dynastic name is Schleswig-Holstein-Sonderburg-Glucksburg, his father's Danish-Greek royal house. But, as a descendant of Queen Victoria as well as earlier monarchs, the Duke of Edinburgh can himself legitimately claim to be a member of the House of Windsor, in its broader meaning.

Finally, the choice of dynastic name does not in fact rest with the predecessor. The Queen has stated her desire and the present legal situation, but it will be up to the Prince of Wales to decide after he becomes King whether to follow her proclamation or to choose one of his father's names through his own proclamation.

When Prince Philip became the consort to a queen on February 6, 1952, all the experiences of four hundred years made one thing completely clear: It was not the titles he would or would not bear that would determine his role, nor would it be the general approval or criticism of his Sovereign's subjects. Philip has now been consort to a queen for longer than any other man in our history and it has been up to him, and him alone, what his legacy will be.

When recording the role that consorts to queens have played in history one must be cautious in making conclusions. A consort's concrete achievements and activities, either as an individual or in unity with

The Duke of Edinburgh has accompanied the Queen on almost all of her tours of Canada and other countries around the world, but also had to establish his own role in the reign of his wife.

his Queen, can be observed and assessed. Where there are diaries or observations by contemporaries, influence can be surmised and lines drawn from a consort to actions by a queen or others. And informed connections can often be made between known beliefs or attitudes and consequent results. But, while a consort may be an adviser, as Prince Albert described himself, his relationship is first of all of another kind. He is a spouse, either through a politically arranged marriage or a love match.

Whether the relationship between spouses is as cold as an Arctic iceberg or as hot as a volcanic island in the Pacific, there is always one common characteristic. Like the iceberg or the island, all that the observer, whether historian or contemporary, every really sees is the tip of the relationship. And even that metaphor fails in that the subaquatic or subterranean bulk beneath the visible point can often be explored, if with difficulty. In the bulk of the human relationship between spouses even the principals involved may not be able to fully articulate or understand the complex dynamics of the partnership. Thus the full influence of a consort on his Queen will always remain a mystery to intrigue their own generation and the generations that follow. It is probably greater than generally credited.

5
Queen, Prince, and People

"We celebrate today a stewardship faithfully exercised by Her Majesty"
— *Right Reverend Alistair Dunlop*

As the British Airways plane came to a halt in Richmond, Virginia, on the occasion of the royal couple's fourth state visit to the United States, the unthinkable happened — or rather, didn't happen. As the red carpet was being wrestled to the tarmac, and a loudspeaker announced, "The Queen has landed," the steps that would allow Her Majesty the Queen and His Royal Highness the Duke of Edinburgh to alight from the airplane and onto American soil were found to be too short and would not immediately align with the door of the aircraft. As a uniformed royal aide stood in the open door for nearly fifteen minutes and calmly gave the workers on the ground hand signals, another man, in suit and tie and looking slightly impatient, emerged from the interior of the aircraft and joined in the efforts to direct the placement of the steps.

This take-charge gesture was typical of Prince Philip. A naval veteran, the Duke's effort was that of a man who values efficiency and is not afraid to muck in and make things happen, regardless of rank. As a husband, this attempt to get the show on the road was a practical gesture of support for his wife and the respect in which he holds both her and her royal role. The thought of the Queen being stranded on the tarmac in front of the assembled members of the world's press must have been an appalling one for her husband. After twenty minutes, the problem was rectified. Featured on the evening newscasts — but not as the main event of the couple's first day in the United States — Philip's efforts added slightly comic colour to yet another royal visit and made him the figure viewers associated with the erstwhile airplane steps, not the Queen.

For most people around the world, a royal visit — especially by Her Majesty the Queen — is cause

The Queen's airplane faced technical problems when it arrived in Richmond, Virginia.

of the founding of Jamestown, America's first English settlement, the Queen was also asked to help the people of the state come to terms with a more recent tragic chapter of their history.

Just over two weeks before her arrival, thirty-two people had been killed and many more injured by a suicidal student gunman at Virginia Polytechnical Institute. Touched by Her Majesty's prompt and heartfelt message of condolence shortly after the tragedy, the state and the people of Virginia gratefully accepted her public and private expressions of sympathy during this visit. At the State Capitol, a guard of honour of eleven military cadets from Virginia Tech stood watch as part of the official welcoming party. The gap in their ranks was an unfilled spot originally intended for Cadet Matthew La Porte, who was one of the students slain. Inside, at a special session of the Virginia General Assembly, the Queen said, "You are still coming to terms with the dreadful events at Virginia Tech. My heart goes out to students, friends and families of those killed and to the many others who have been affected, some of whom I will be meeting shortly. On behalf of the people of the United Kingdom, I extend my deepest sympathies at this time of such grief and sorrow."

Away from the cameras, Her Majesty met privately with students and faculty, among them Kathleen Carney, who was shot in the hand. She presented the Queen with a bracelet in Virginia Tech colours — maroon and orange — and featuring thirty-two stones, in honour of the fallen. Although the Queen's response to this touching gesture remains unreported, the act itself echoes the presentation to her of the police badge of deceased

for great excitement and curiosity. No matter how jaded members of the public profess to be prior to a royal engagement, a chance to see Her Majesty or a member of her family in the flesh is an opportunity few pass up. That day in May 2007, the people of Virginia seized their chance, as they lined the rainy streets of Richmond to watch the royal couple make their way to the Virginia General Assembly. Although the visit to Virginia was originally planned as a commemoration of the four hundredth anniversary

The Queen and Duke of Edinburgh ride through historic Williamsburg, second capital of Virginia, in a carriage in 2007 as they celebrate the four hundredth anniversary of English settlement in the United States.

thirty-four-year-old New York police detective Joseph Vigrano. Vigrano and his firefighter brother, John, both willingly sacrificed their lives in an attempt to save others in New York City's World Trade Center during the terrorist attacks of September 11, 2001. This gift to the Queen was in appreciation of Britain's support for America in the aftermath of the atrocities of that devastating day.

Among the messages the Queen sent to America regarding the attacks was one sent to the memorial service for British victims held at St. Thomas Church in New York. In it, she wrote, "These are dark and

The Duke of Edinburgh boards a replica of the Susan Constant, *one of three vessels that brought settlers to Jamestown in 1607.*

harrowing times for families and friends of those who are missing or who suffered in the attack, many of you here today. My thoughts and prayers are with you all now and in the difficult days ahead. But nothing that can be said can begin to take away the anguish and pain of these moments; grief is the price we pay for love."

In 1996, on Mothering Sunday, the Queen and the Princess Royal visited Dunblane, Scotland, the site of a horrific primary school shooting in which the victims were schoolchildren aged five and six and their teachers. On this occasion — only four days after the massacre of these tiny innocents that devastated the small Scottish town — the royal mother and daughter attended a memorial service and met privately and tearfully with the bereaved and the injured.

Aware that the Crown is a rallying point during both tragic and triumphant times, the Queen does her duty seriously and without vanity. Her intention

The Queen and the Princess Royal visit Dunblane, Scotland, in the wake of the tragedy there. The snowdrop was a symbol of grief in the village. In response, the Princess Royal laid a simple posy of snowdrops from her garden.

is never to interfere or seek the spotlight, but instead to be a help rather than a hindrance. In 1966, this attitude was sorely tested when she did not immediately make her way to the mining village of Aberfan in Wales, the site of a massive collapse of a slag heap that caused the deaths of 144 people, most of them children attending the local school, which was engulfed by hundreds of thousands of tons of rubble. Concerned that any appearance by her — no matter how low-key — would shift resources from the rescue and recovery effort, the Duke of Edinburgh and Lord Snowdon went to the site of the tragedy as representatives of the Crown. The intent was that the Queen would visit when it was certain she would not be an unwelcome and potentially dangerous distraction. However, at a time when hundreds of her subjects grabbed shovels, hopped in their cars, and rushed to the village in a heartfelt and impulsive attempt to assist in the rescue effort, her absence in the immediate aftermath of the tragedy was viewed as deeply suspect in some circles. Months later, as she surveyed the site of the disaster and met with dozens of bereaved parents, she acknowledged that as their monarch and as a parent herself, she felt their loss keenly, telling them sincerely, "I'm sorry, but I can give you nothing at present except sympathy."

The Queen visits Aberfan, South Wales, in October 1966. Of the 144 people killed, most were children. As Queen and parent, she privately told bereaved mothers and fathers, "I can give you nothing at present except sympathy."

respected, and often beloved, public figure, she has recently been targeted for assassination by the terrorist group al-Qaeda, not because she is so well known but because she is seen by them as the "crusader Queen." Her credibility as guardian of Christianity in Britain poses a very real threat to their wish to impose their religious agenda upon the West. As author Melanie Phillips writes in her 2006 book, *Londonistan*:

> Al-Qaeda, of course, does not see the established church as an anachronism at all. On the contrary, since … it treats religion with the utmost seriousness, it understands very well the crucial significance of Christianity in the life of the British nation. Dethrone Christianity, and the job of subjugating the West is halfway done. That's why al-Qaeda has specifically targeted the "crusader" Queen for assassination.

This humble yet heartfelt response is typical of the Queen's lack of both pretension and presumption. Naturally shy and somewhat self-contained, her personality and her conduct remain reliable and constant, and she is viewed as a seemingly unchanging touchstone in a turbulent world. Supreme Governor of the Church of England and bearer of the solemn title "Defender of the Faith," the Queen takes this role, as well as her Christian beliefs, very seriously. Although she is seen by nations and individuals throughout the world as a politically uncontroversial and universally

The late Queen Mother was viewed by Adolf Hitler as "the most dangerous woman in Europe," and her elder daughter must also frustrate this latest threat to decency and humanity. While she is a committed Christian, the Queen reigns over the peaceful and pluralistic Commonwealth. She is welcomed as a visitor throughout the world to countries populated by people of all faiths. At home, she has made religious history as a monarch, receiving Pope John Paul II at Buckingham Palace in 1982 — the first Pope to visit in 450 years. She has also visited a U.K. mosque (in Lincolnshire) and has incorporated a prayer room in Windsor

Castle, thereby granting a request made by Muslim members of her staff employed there.

On the morning of July 7, 2005, terrorists finally made good their threat to attack London. Four suicide bombers made their way onto three underground trains and one double-decker bus. By the time they had completed their deadly mission, fifty-two people were dead and seven hundred were injured. The next day, members of the Royal Family, led by the Queen, visited the injured in hospitals throughout the city. After her visit to the wounded survivors at London's Whitechapel Royal Hospital, Her Majesty, with a slightly quavering voice, gave a forthright and determined message to her subjects:

I want to express my admiration for the people of our capital city who in the aftermath of yesterday's bombings are calmly determined to resume their normal lives.

This is the answer to this outrage. Sadly we in Britain have been all too familiar with acts of terror and members of my generation, especially at this end of London, know that we have been here before.

But those who perpetuate these brutal acts against innocent people should know that they will not change our way of life.

Atrocities such as these simply reinforce our sense of community, our humanity and our trust in the rule of law. That is the clear message from us all.

Royal aides told the assembled press that it was unusual for the Queen to speak so soon after an incident, while one veteran journalist insisted that the uncharacteristic quaver in the Queen's voice that day was not due to sorrow but rather an indication of "incandescent anger." Whatever the cause, a week later when London and parts of the world came to a standstill for a two-minute silence in honour of the victims and in defiance of the terrorists, the enduring image was not of the countless cabs and buses coming to a standstill, nor of the thousands of ordinary people halting during the day, nor even of the Mayor, the Prime Minister, or the many celebrities standing side by side in solidarity. Impressive as those sights were, it was the small figure clad in pink and carrying a seemingly ever-present handbag standing alone in front of Buckingham Palace for the entire two

The Queen speaks to Sister Mary Lawrence, a Catholic nun at Royal London Hospital, where victims of the July 7, 2005, terrorist attack were treated.

minutes that remained in the hearts and minds of her people.

From an early age, the Queen was trained to be an effective monarch and knew that her destiny would be a somewhat solitary calling. However, she touchingly paid tribute to Prince Philip and his role as her staunchest supporter when on the occasion of their golden wedding anniversary she said her husband had been her "strength and stay all these years." It is natural that the aforementioned demands of public life would tax even the most balanced and disciplined person, as the Queen most certainly is. Nevertheless, the strains and stresses of the job are easier to bear with the Duke as her faithful consort and supportive husband.

In addition to fulfilling these roles, Prince Philip is also responsible for balancing the Queen's respect for tradition with an understanding for the necessity of progress, resulting in many royal firsts. Early in her reign, on the Duke's suggestion, the Queen discontinued the presentation of debutantes at court. Instead, the royal couple introduced small, informal luncheons in order to meet a larger — and in many cases, more accomplished — cross-section of British society, a tradition that began in 1956 and continues today. Another tradition initiated by the Queen and Prince Philip, which endures, is the royal walkabout. Today, walkabouts are an integral part of royal visits, and their roots are found in the King and Queen mingling with veterans at the unveiling of the National War Memorial in Ottawa in 1939, but the first official walkabout took place in 1970 during the Queen and the Duke of Edinburgh's tour of Australia and New Zealand, yet another effort by the couple to meet a greater

The Queen waves farewell after visiting the Hospital for Sick Children in Great Ormond Street, London, early in her reign.

number and variety of people, not simply those in receiving lines.

Although he has accompanied the Queen on all of her Commonwealth tours and state visits, as well as on engagements throughout the United Kingdom, Prince Philip has also carved out a productive role for himself within the strictures of royal life. While on a tour of the Commonwealth in 1952 and acting as a substitute for her father, Princess Elizabeth —

The Queen and Prince Philip on one of their frequent royal walkabouts, this time in Canada.

accompanied by her husband on the visit — sat on the platform of the Treetops Hotel in Kenya. Tucked in the branches of a giant fig tree and unbeknownst to her at the time, Princess Elizabeth became Queen Elizabeth II. As Countess Mountbatten of Burma, Elizabeth and Philip's mutual cousin, said, "She went up as a Princess and came down a Queen."

Although the King had been unwell, his sudden death on February 6 was nevertheless a shock to the young couple. Elizabeth's accession to the Throne came far sooner than the couple had imagined, even though the King's ill health had resulted in Philip giving up his naval career because of Princess Elizabeth's increasing royal responsibilities.

Although Philip's wife was now the Queen, he had no political role upon her accession to the Throne and no recent role model as husband to a monarch. (The last male consort had been Queen Victoria's beloved Prince Albert.) As he told biographer Gyles Brandreth, "I had to find a way of supporting the Queen, without getting in the way … I had to fit in. I had to avoid getting at cross-purposes, usurping others' authority. In most cases that was no problem. I did my own thing."

"Doing his own thing" has culminated in a royal career that has resulted in Prince Philip's patronage or presidency of more than eight hundred organizations and charities. According to Buckingham Palace, by the time he had reached his early eighties, the Duke of Edinburgh had fulfilled more than twenty thousand official engagements. His first appointment came a year after his marriage, when in 1948 he was appointed President of the National Playing Fields Association. Wisely, King George VI realized that his ambitious and energetic son-in-law would need something of significance to do, as, with the King's death, Philip's responsibility to Elizabeth and the Crown would grow and any advancement of his naval career would be hindered, rather than helped, by his elevated royal status.

Philip worked hard mounting appeals, finding

Princess Elizabeth became Queen Elizabeth II in Treetops Hotel in Kenya on February 6, 1952.

seamlessly transferred his enthusiasm and capacity for hard work from the role of naval officer to that of royal benefactor with no regrets. However, that would probably not be accurate.

Never one to moan, Prince Philip got on with the inevitable in typically stoic fashion, eventually taking on no more active naval appointments from July 1951. However, he was quoted as once saying, "I wanted none of it. I never sought any of it. Not the position or the appointments I received. They were invitations. It was not my ambition to be President of the Mint Advisory Committee or President of the World Wide Fund for Nature. I'd much rather have stayed in the Navy, frankly."

This type of comment is rare and probably made from a frustrated and defensive position. Royal by birth and by inclination, the Duke, like the Queen, is not quick to complain or explain. Rather, both are known for their sense of duty.

The Duke's responsibilities are an eclectic collection of concerns that echo his wide range of interests. Two organizations that he is heavily involved with are the aforementioned World Wide Fund for Nature (WWF) and his creation, the Duke of Edinburgh's Award Scheme. Philip has a keen interest in the environment, underscored by his long-standing involvement with the WWF. Since 1961, he has been much more than a figurehead, visiting WWF projects in forty countries on five continents. Long before it became fashionable, the Duke had a passionate interest in conservation. According to Buckingham Palace, the Duke, described as a "committed and enquiring Christian," has even composed a prayer documenting his interest in the relationship between natural science and faith:

donors, and even starring in a film with Bob Hope about poor postwar children in London whose only playgrounds were the streets. This trailblazing effort alone raised £84,000. The young Duke soon found himself travelling thousands of miles each year in aid of this, his first charitable appointment, saying, "I will go anywhere to open a playing field." His early and encouraging success in this endeavour might lead one to believe that the Duke of Edinburgh

O Lord, the creator of the universe and author of the laws of nature, inspire in us thy servants the will to ensure the survival of all the species of animals and plants, which you have given to share this planet with us. Help us to understand that we have a responsibility for them and that "having dominion" does not mean that you have given us the right to exploit the living world without thought for the consequences. Through him who taught us that Solomon in all his glory could not compare with the beauty of the flowers in the field.

This idealistic and socially concerned side of the Duke is also in evidence when he presents Duke of Edinburgh's Awards to youth throughout the world. Founded by the Prince in 1956, the "Dukes" are a "voluntary, non-competitive and flexible programme of cultural and adventurous activities for all young people, whatever their background or ability."

When he formed the organization, the Duke of Edinburgh was adamant that anyone participating in the awards scheme did so out of "free choice." Available to young people age fourteen to twenty-five, participants can now be found in more than one hundred countries, and at any given time about 250,000 youth around the world are working towards attaining their awards. The programme is tailored to each individual, regardless of circumstances — especially the physical component, with one severely disabled participant determinedly walking

The Duke of Edinburgh touring an underground mining pit.

three city blocks using crutches in order to complete his award requirements.

One of the most well known Gold Award Achievers is Prince Edward. The Earl of Wessex now also travels the globe in aid of the organization,

The Duke of Edinburgh visited the Reifel Island Migratory Bird Sanctuary in Delta, British Columbia, in March 1992 as part of the World Wildlife Fund's Spring Birdathon fundraiser.

Prince Philip presenting Gold Awards to participants in the Duke of Edinburgh's Award Programme in Alberta, 1992.

both fundraising and presiding over many awards ceremonies. To the press, Duke of Edinburgh's Awards ceremonies are a source of happy, often touching human interest stories and predictable photo opportunities. The achievers are impressive young people with uplifting and often heart-rending stories. The picture opportunities, however, make it clear whom the ceremony is for. Whether it is the Duke of Edinburgh or his son at the podium, they are all too aware that this is one of the most important days of each participant's life thus far. Therefore, they have a word with each one and stand still for a carefully composed handshake picture. After the ceremony, the Princes make an effort to speak informally to the achievers and their families. While the royal men tolerate the presence of the press, they seem oblivious to them, instead concentrating on making the day truly memorable for the young people they have come to honour.

Throughout the fifty-year history of the awards, the Duke has worked tirelessly to expand their reach. In its golden jubilee year, new participants could be found in Native communities in the Canadian North, in the inner cities of the United Kingdom, and in centres for young offenders, some in Canada.

While the Duke could take great satisfaction in his namesake organization as it reached its fiftieth year, the Queen's Golden Jubilee year in 2002 set the stage for royal celebrations throughout the United Kingdom and the Commonwealth. Following the traumatic death of Diana, Princess of Wales, in 1997 and more immediately the deaths of her sister, Princess Margaret, and Queen Elizabeth the Queen Mother in early 2002, Her Majesty could be forgiven for thinking her Jubilee celebrations might have a somewhat muted tone. Even some sections of the media, led by the left-leaning *Guardian* newspaper, predicted a lacklustre event, largely ignored by an apathetic public.

Australian and Bahamian first day covers marking the Queen's Golden Jubilee featured images of the Queen and the Duke of Edinburgh throughout her reign.

The Queen began her official Jubilee year by marking the anniversary of her father's death and her own accession — usually a day of quiet reflection — by visiting a cancer care unit in King's Lynn, Norfolk. Beginning her Jubilee year in this way was entirely appropriate and not at all sombre. Instead, the Queen was photographed smiling broadly and wearing bright green as she chatted with patients and staff.

On April 29, she dined at Number 10 Downing Street, in the presence of her living British Prime Ministers — Tony Blair, John Major, Margaret Thatcher, and Edward Heath, Tony Blair having been born during her reign. The next day, Her Majesty addressed what she called "the Mother of Parliaments" and stated she was confident that the "timeless values" would continue to guide future generations, whatever the future might hold. "These enduring British traditions and values — moderation, openness, tolerance, service — have stood the test of time, and I am convinced they will stand us in good stead in the future," she said.

The Queen and the Duke of Edinburgh began their exhaustive three-month Golden Jubilee tour of the United Kingdom on May 1. Inside the Guildhall in Bath, the Queen expressed her gratitude to the people who turned out to welcome her and those who had shown their support throughout her reign, especially during her recent bereavements: "I would like to thank all those who have made the last two days so enjoyable. Following a time of sadness in my family, the warmth of the welcome we have received in the southwest has been especially heartening. Your celebration of my reign has brought home to me with renewed force how much I owe to you all for your loyalty over the last half century."

In Belfast's St. Anne's Cathedral, a multi-denominational church service was held during which the Right Reverend Alistair Dunlop paid tribute to the Queen with these words: "Stewardship, grace, trust. Here are key words as, along with the rest of the nation and Commonwealth, we in Northern Ireland celebrate this Jubilee year. We celebrate today a stewardship faithfully exercised by Her Majesty throughout these fifty years."

In Scotland, the Right Reverend John Miller gave thanks for her long reign, describing her as a "beacon of stability, a unifying influence in a world of change." In addition to supporting the Queen during her Jubilee tour, the Duke of Edinburgh presented Duke of Edinburgh's Awards in many of the communities they visited.

On the way to Wick, one of the most northerly towns on the Scottish mainland, the Queen's Flight took time to fly over the Castle of Mey — the much-loved home of the late Queen Elizabeth the Queen Mother. Staff at the castle had constructed a "Happy Jubilee" message in a nearby field visible from the air. The plane circled the site twice, so the Queen could see this touching tribute.

Throughout 2002, there were many glittering events in London to mark the Queen's Golden Jubilee. However, the most impressive and inclusive was the Golden Jubilee Weekend, held June 1 to 4. This event brought people from around the world to London and was viewed by millions more on television. The weekend's inaugural event, "Prom at the Palace," was the biggest gathering ever held in the gardens of Buckingham Palace. With 12,500 attendees, it trumped all garden parties, which usually have a guest list of about 3,000 people. Those lucky enough to secure a ticket were randomly selected from a pool of 2 million applicants from throughout the United Kingdom. In addition to being serenaded by superstars of the worlds of opera and classical music — among them, singer Dame Kiri Te Kanawa and cellist Mstislav Rostropovich — the audience members were treated to a picnic. Presented in a specially commissioned cool bag, the picnic menu included Jubilee Chicken, salmon roulade, shortbread biscuits, strawberries and cream, miniature chocolates, and a half-bottle of champagne!

At the conclusion of the evening, joined by nearly the entire Royal Family — with the exception of the Duke of York, who was on official business in Japan — the audience applauded and cheered for the Queen. Her Majesty and the Duke of Edinburgh then took the performers outside to the forecourt of the palace to greet the crowds gathered around the Queen Victoria Memorial and down the Mall.

The following day, members of the Royal Family dispersed throughout the United Kingdom to attend a few of the many services of thanksgiving taking place in honour of the Queen's fifty years as monarch. More than two thousand well-wishers greeted Her Majesty and Prince Philip at St. George's Chapel, Windsor. While the Prince of Wales, accompanied by Princes William and Harry, attended church in Cardiff, the Princess Royal travelled to Ayr and the Duke of Kent represented the Queen in Belfast.

Buckingham Palace was the focus of massive celebrations of the Queen's Golden Jubilee in daylight and at night.

Back in London, preparations were underway for a celebration that would probably appeal to the young Princes more than it would their ever-dutiful grandmother. Like "Prom at the Palace," "Party at the Palace" hosted some twelve thousand lucky revellers, who were treated to the same celebratory picnic their fellow music lovers had enjoyed at the earlier event. They also had four hours in which to picnic and relax in the Buckingham Palace gardens before the festivities formally got underway. The Duke of York, back from Japan, could be seen with his daughters, Princesses Beatrice and Eugenie, chatting with some of the picnickers as they took in this most unusual sight.

An unorthodox but entirely appropriate version of "God Save the Queen" was performed by rock guitarist Brian May, formerly of the aptly named band Queen. May performed this very special electric guitar solo from the rooftop of Buckingham Palace, visible not only to the massive crowd in the palace gardens but also to the million spectators gathered in the Mall and the millions more throughout the world watching the event on television. The concert was designed to showcase the evolution of popular music throughout the Queen's reign. A few of the featured performers were Tony Bennett, Ozzy Osbourne, Tom Jones, Sir Paul McCartney, and Brian Wilson. Wilson, founder of the American group the Beach Boys, wore a sober blue suit and tie as a gesture of respect for the Queen and the occasion. In the presence of a full retinue of royals, Australian comedian Barry Humphries, as Dame Edna Everage, irreverently welcomed the Queen to the concert, referring to her as "the Jubilee Girl."

At the concert's conclusion, the Prince of Wales addressed the Queen with affection, calling her "Your Majesty," followed quickly by "Mummy," saying, "We feel proud of you — proud and grateful for everything you have done for your country and the Commonwealth for over fifty extraordinary years." He also thanked Prince Philip for his unfailing support, concluding, "You have been a beacon of stability in the midst of profound, sometimes perilous change."

Accompanied by her husband, the Queen lit the final beacon in a chain that stretched around the world, a replication of events of the last Golden Jubilee, that of Queen Victoria in 1887.

Although the Queen and the Duke of Edinburgh would undertake visits to the Commonwealth countries of Jamaica, New Zealand, Australia, and Canada throughout 2002, the Commonwealth also featured prominently on the last day of the Golden Jubilee Weekend in London. With many spectators camping out for several days to ensure a coveted viewing spot, more than a million people — many of them waving flags from Commonwealth countries — lined the streets of London to see the Queen and the Duke of Edinburgh travel in the Gold State Coach from Buckingham Palace to St. Paul's Cathedral for the National Service of Thanksgiving for the Queen's reign. Later, the weekend's finale was a spectacular parade made up of more than twenty thousand performers embodying six themes of the Jubilee — service, community, thanksgiving, celebration, past and future, and the Commonwealth. More than four thousand people from the fifty-three countries of the Commonwealth participated in the colourful procession and declared their loyalty to the Queen via four thousand hand-drawn messages that arrived at Buckingham Palace on a massive banner.

The Commonwealth is dear to the Queen's heart, although many of her Prime Ministers in the United Kingdom have failed to understand its relevance to her. A voluntary association of independent states, of which Her Majesty is Head, the Commonwealth is composed mostly of countries that made up the former British Empire. One notable exception is Mozambique, a former Portuguese colony, which joined the Commonwealth in 1995. Countries that have withdrawn from the Commonwealth are few. South Africa withdrew from the organization in 1961 but rejoined in 1994, after Nelson Mandela became President. With more than 2 billion citizens and accounting for over 30 percent of the world's population, the Queen takes her position as Head of the Commonwealth very seriously. On the final day of the Golden Jubilee celebrations in London, she included the Commonwealth in her message of thanks, saying, "Gratitude, respect and pride, these words sum up how I feel about the people of this country and the Commonwealth — and what this Golden Jubilee means to me."

Since her Golden Jubilee, both the Queen and the Duke of Edinburgh have tirelessly continued to do their duty, the most recent overseas trip being their state visit to America, where they toured the states of Virginia, Kentucky, and the District of Columbia. Although the Queen fulfilled a lifelong dream while there to attend the Kentucky Derby, both she and the Duke carried out a full

Unveiling of a coin featuring the Queen's image on the obverse by the Royal Canadian Mint.

programme of engagements with no concession to their age. This earned them the respect and admiration of the American public and of the American President. By the time he had reached his second term in office, George W. Bush had hosted many state dinners. However, the only people for whom he agreed to don white tie and tails were the Queen and Prince Philip, hosting his first — and likely only — fully formal state dinner in their honour.

During the Jubilee, the Queen issued a personal thank you to her husband and children for the contribution they have made to her life and to the Monarchy:

> I take this opportunity to mention the strength I draw from my own family. The Duke of Edinburgh has made an invaluable contribution to my life over these past fifty years, as he has to so many charities and organizations with which he has been involved.

We both of us have a special place in our hearts for our children. I want to express my admiration for the Prince of Wales and for all he has achieved for this country. Our children, and all my family, have given me such love and unstinting help over the years, and especially in recent months.

6 Managing the Family Firm

"If you are really going to have a monarchy,
you have got to have a family, and the family has got to be in the public eye"

— Prince Philip, Duke of Edinburgh

The Queen and Prince Philip's sixty years of married life and equally steadfast decades of royal service have produced a family whose personal lives are more a reflection of contemporary life than their parents' example. The Royal Family is like no other family, yet it mirrors the lives of many modern families throughout the United Kingdom and the Commonwealth. Three out of four of the Queen and the Duke of Edinburgh's children are divorced, two have remarried, and two have married members of the middle-class rather than the aristocracy or the gentry. In addition to her personal role as mother to four and grandmother to seven, the Queen must act as an example to her eventual successors, future kings the Prince of Wales and his elder son, Prince William.

The Duke of Edinburgh has said, "Monarchy involves the whole family, which means that different age groups are part of it. There are people who can look, for instance, at the Queen Mother and identify with that generation, or with us or with our children." Walter Bagehot, the Victorian constitutionalist who famously warned about the peril of "letting daylight in upon the magic," wrote, "A family on the Throne … brings down the pride of sovereignty to the level of petty life." Each of these statements can be applied to the Queen's family and the effects their actions have had on her reign.

Philip's father, Prince Andrew, died before his son's marriage to Elizabeth. However, Philip and his wife were able to enjoy a close relationship with his mother, Princess Alice, when she lived with them in

The members of their extended family posed with the Queen and the Duke after Her Majesty's Coronation.

Buckingham Palace. Both Princess Alice's failing health and the April 1967 coup in Greece were behind the invitation "from Lilibet personally" to live with Philip and her in London. Princess Alice had founded a small religious order and was most often attired in traditional habit and wimple, with a crucifix worn around her neck. Viewed by many as eccentric, the Princess had by then overcome her mental illness and had emerged from the war years as a woman of courage and character. At great risk to herself, the Princess had hidden a Jewish family in her home in Greece, ultimately saving their lives, during the Second World War. Her discretion and deep religious faith were also appreciated by her daughter-in-law, with whom she enjoyed a relaxed and unguarded relationship. She died in her sleep

at Buckingham Palace on December 5, 1969, aged eighty-four.

Prince Philip and the Queen also extended this sense of family loyalty to his sisters. His sister Cecile died with her husband and children, as the result of a tragic plane crash, in 1937, when Philip was only seventeen. His remaining siblings — Margarita, Theodora, and Sophie — who all lived in Germany, have since died. During their lives, Philip kept in regular touch with them, both before and after the Second World War, although his royal duties affected how and when he was able to see them. His sisters, all living in Germany and married to Germans — some with controversial war records — were not invited to his wedding. When his sister Theodora died in 1963, the Prince was on an official visit to Canada

Princess Elizabeth was trained by her father King George VI to be Sovereign, as on this occasion at Royal Lodge, Windsor, in 1942.

Princess Alice, mother of the Duke of Edinburgh, established her own Orthodox religious order of nuns.

and the United States and decided that he could not interrupt the tour in order to attend her funeral. Nevertheless, the Duke's sisters were in attendance at the Coronation and often stayed with him and the Queen in Scotland.

Prince Philip's practical approach to royal life is often at odds with the attitude of his eldest son, the Prince of Wales. The Duke told Gyles Brandreth that he and Charles have "one great difference. He's a romantic — I'm a pragmatist. That means we do see things differently. And because I don't see things as a romantic would, I'm unfeeling."

Charles Philip Arthur George was born on November 14, 1948, nearly a year after his parents' wedding, in Buckingham Palace. His birth was soon followed by that of his sister, Anne, on August 15, 1950. Their mother was not yet Queen, so they were raised like many other aristocratic children — nannies were employed and the nursery routine was sacrosanct.

The Prince of Wales and the Princess Royal at an Order of the Garter ceremony at Windsor Castle.

Princess Elizabeth, typical of her class and time, was a traditionalist who, in private, deferred to the wishes of her husband and viewed him as head of the home. While the King was physically well, the Princess was able to experience the closest she would ever come to a truly private life, as a naval wife in Malta, when Philip was posted there. During this period, the Princess alternated time in Malta with time in England. When she was in Malta, the infant Prince Charles was left in the care of his devoted nannies and equally devoted grandparents.

As her father's health deteriorated, the Princess was called upon more frequently to act on his behalf. In 1952, when she became Queen, the time she was able to spend with her children was lessened as she adapted to and adopted her new and onerous responsibilities, leaving Prince Philip and often the Queen Mother with increased responsibility for Charles and Anne. The births of the Princes Andrew and Edward, in 1960 and 1964 respectively, came at a time when the Queen had settled into her duties. While Charles and Anne's upbringing had been interrupted by Elizabeth's elevation to monarch from mother, Andrew and Edward were beneficiaries of a more relaxed approach by their parents to childrearing. Not only were they now more experienced as parents, but also the Queen had mastered her role as monarch. While this did not mean her responsibilities were lessened, it did mean that she was now comfortable and confident in her role and could perhaps more actively enjoy this second chance at motherhood.

While Princess Anne seemed to possess a strong and robust character much like that of her father, Prince Charles was a far more sensitive child and

Princess Anne was christened in the White Drawing Room of Buckingham Palace, October 21, 1950.

suffered for it during his boyhood, by his own account. The silver lining in this childhood cloud was his relationship with his grandmother, Queen Elizabeth the Queen Mother. Seemingly kindred spirits, the Prince's grand style of living is more in tune with her sensibilities than those of his parents. On the death of the Queen Mother, the Prince of Wales praised her, saying, "She was quite simply the most magical grandmother you could possibly have and I was utterly devoted to her. For me, she meant everything, and I have dreaded, dreaded this moment."

The Prince has also spoken publicly about his parents, when in June 1994 he granted his authorized biographer, Jonathan Dimbleby, access for a book and television interview. He made it clear that his childhood had been a very unhappy one. He told Dimbleby and the world that he was "emotionally estranged" from his parents and craved "the affection and appreciation" that they were either "unable or unwilling" to give

In 1986 the Prince and Princess of Wales visited Vancouver, British Columbia. The breakdown of their marriage was played out in the glare of media attention.

him, leaving him feeling neglected. He gave the impression that his mother was uncaring and distant and that his father was bullying and insensitive. These revelations coincided with an historic visit the Queen was making to Russia. The Queen made no comment, but the Duke simply told reporters who asked for a comment on the Dimbleby book, "I've never discussed private matters, and I don't think the Queen has either. I've never made any comment about any member of the family in forty years, and I'm not going to start now."

As controversial as the public airing of his childhood sorrows by the Prince of Wales was, the most shocking part of the interview was his public admission of adultery, which he said had occurred only after the marriage had "irretrievably broken down — both of us having tried." In Charles's defence, he spoke out in a misguided but well-intentioned attempt to end speculation about his troubled marriage to Diana, mother of his two sons. For the Queen and Prince Philip, this was yet another in a series of sad and sometimes salacious events that had seemingly engulfed the Royal Family since their children had become adults.

By no means a complete summary of their family's misadventures, the Queen's self-professed "annus horribilis" — 1992 — provides a sad commentary of the personal missteps of her three eldest children and their spouses. Princess Anne's divorce from Captain Mark Phillips, the Duke and Duchess of York's separation, and the ongoing and very public acrimony between the Prince and Princess of Wales must have been extremely disappointing for the Queen and the Duke of Edinburgh, both personally and professionally. In addition, the ever-increasing media attention the family endured was complicated by the fact that one of their own — the Princess of Wales — had co-operated with former tabloid journalist Andrew Morton in the writing of an exposé entitled *Diana: Her True Story*. Prince Philip, an admittedly far less patient person than the Queen, was infuriated with what he saw as a betrayal by the Princess and snubbed her at Royal Ascot that year. The Queen, a more conservative character, repeatedly urged the couple to take a wait-and-see attitude in the hopes that they could patch up their troubled union, if only for the sake of their sons, William and Harry. Both she and the Duke had naturally hoped that all of their children would enjoy successful marriages and bring their children up in traditional, intact homes.

The Queen's second son, Prince Andrew, the Duke of York, with Sarah, Duchess of York, in front of Niagara Falls, Ontario, in 1987. Their marriage too would fail.

The Queen's seemingly endless patience was eventually exhausted, however, with the antics of both the Duchess of York and the Princess of Wales. Although it is impossible to know what Her Majesty thought of the photographic evidence of the Duchess's relationship with American John Bryan, after the television interview the Princess of Wales granted the BBC's *Panorama* — in which she also admitted adultery and questioned her husband's fitness as future King — the Queen had letters hand-delivered to both of the Waleses, suggesting they divorce as soon as possible.

The Princess Royal in Nova Scotia on one of her many tours around the Commonwealth on behalf of her mother, the Queen.

Even after the divorces of Andrew and Charles, the Queen kept the lines of communication open with her former daughters-in-law, although Prince Philip has taken a harsher view — especially concerning the Duchess of York. Out of the three broken unions, Princess Anne's was, unsurprisingly, the least complicated. Her subsequent remarriage to the Queen's equerry, Captain Timothy Laurence, presented a slight hiccup. Keeping in mind

The Queen's youngest son, Prince Edward, at a Duke of Edinburgh's Awards press conference at Government House in Edmonton, Alberta, Canada, in 1993 (top) and, having been made the Earl of Wessex, with the Countess following their wedding.

the Queen's position as Supreme Governor of the Church of England, the divorced Princess Royal and her second husband were married in a quiet family ceremony at the Presbyterian Crathie Church, near Balmoral Castle in Scotland.

This wedding was unusual by royal standards. Princess Anne's first wedding — like those of Charles and Diana and Andrew and Sarah — was a romantic and elaborate ceremonial in which the couple rode in horse-drawn carriages through the streets of London, the entire spectacle viewed by thousands on the streets of the city and millions throughout the world via their television sets. However, the subsequent breakdowns of these unions led the Royal Family to rethink the presentation of these important family and monarchical occasions. The wedding of Princess Anne and Captain Laurence was entirely appropriate, and even if she could have had a grander wedding the second time around, it is doubtful the Princess would have considered such an idea.

The wedding of Prince Edward and Sophie Rhys-Jones called for an entirely different approach. Although the royal weddings were presumably being scaled down in response to the dissolution of the marriages of the Queen and the Duke's three oldest children, this was Edward and Sophie's first (and hopefully only) wedding, and they deserved a suitable pageant. The result was a wedding at St. George's Chapel, Windsor, with no state or ceremonial involvement, but still a glittering guest list, ladies in long dresses, and a carriage ride by the couple after the ceremony to satisfy the thousands of well-wishers and media gathered at Windsor Castle.

Another wedding in Windsor that required a new template was that of the divorced and then widowed Prince of Wales and the divorced and controversial Camilla Parker Bowles in Windsor on April 9, 2005. The couple married in a civil ceremony in Windsor's Guildhall. Almost every member of the Royal Family was in attendance, except the Queen and the Duke of Edinburgh. Mindful of her position in the Church of England, Her Majesty and Prince Philip did, however, attend the larger service of blessing led by the Archbishop of Canterbury and held at Windsor Castle. In her motherly capacity, the Queen also hosted the wedding reception and made an affectionate speech, declaring that she was "proud" of her son and wished him and his wife — now Her Royal Highness the Duchess of Cornwall — well.

Although the Queen aptly compartmentalized her personal and monarchical roles on such a potentially problematic occasion, she and the Duke — and perhaps the entire institution of monarchy — were grossly misunderstood on the shocking and tragic death of Diana, Princess of Wales. The death of the young and vibrant Princess in a crumpled car in a Paris underpass happened in the early hours of August 31, 1997, while most of the continent was asleep. The Queen, the Queen Mother, the Prince of Wales, and the two young Princes, William and Harry, were at Balmoral for their annual summer retreat. The first call stating that the Princess was injured was unsettling enough, but when subsequent calls determined that the Princess had died from her injuries, the Royal Family was as shocked as any of their fellow countrymen.

The first priority was the well-being of the young Princes. Admittedly, the press photos of the boys attending church that same day with no mention of their deceased mother at any time during the service made for terrible public relations, but their father's family is not heartless. The boys were not forced to attend church; they chose to do so, although they may have done so in a state of shock. As well, the Queen and her mother are and were avowed Christians, and church certainly would be a natural place for each of them to seek solace. William and Harry's behaviour in the difficult time that followed reflects that they have been raised to forge ahead stoically, even during the most trying circumstances.

The Queen and the Duke of Edinburgh's cousin, Countess Mountbatten of Burma, says that the Queen was acting as a loving and responsible grandmother by staying in Scotland and not immediately rushing down to London in the aftermath of Diana's death:

> There she was a grandmother with her grandchildren up in Scotland where they were away from the pressures of the media and the crowds, I mean, wouldn't that be the perfect place to be? Why should you have to come back to a lot of mostly young people?
>
> If she had taken these children whose mother had just died and rushed down into the crowd in London, it would be absolutely against any grandmother's sense of responsibility, or to leave them [without her] up at Balmoral.

That episode in history was chronicled in the motion picture *The Queen*. Her portrayal of the Monarch garnered Dame Helen Mirren an

Academy Award for Best Actress. Of the film, Countess Mountbatten (whose late husband Lord Brabourne was a highly successful film producer) says, "I thought it was very good. I think Helen Mirren was fantastic in being able to portray very exactly the Queen's character and the problems that faced them … the British public becoming sort of hysterical, very odd."

The Countess's opinion was confirmed when the demands of royal duty fell on the boyish shoulders of fifteen-year-old Prince William and thirteen-year-old Prince Harry, as they accompanied their father on a sombre walkabout in front of Kensington Palace. Faced by wailing and weeping crowds — the majority of whom had never met their mother — they comported themselves with dignity and grace. William, even managing to smile and thank people for coming, demonstrated true nobility. He carried out

The Duke of Edinburgh accompanied Prince William, Earl Spencer, Prince Harry, and the Prince of Wales at the funeral of Diana, Princess of Wales.

one excruciating public appearance associated with his mother's death with the aid of his grandfather, the Duke of Edinburgh. Diana's brother, Earl Spencer; the Prince of Wales; and Charles and Diana's sons were meant to walk behind the gun carriage carrying the Princess's coffin along the funeral route. William, a shy teenager, felt he wasn't able to do so. Fearing that he would someday regret this decision, Prince Philip offered to walk alongside him. William, who reportedly adores his grandfather, agreed to walk in the procession on the condition that the Duke accompany him. As the sad procession passed under Admiralty Arch, the Duke could be seen briefly putting a comforting arm across his grandson's shoulders.

On her twenty-fifth wedding anniversary, the Queen stated, "A marriage begins by joining man and wife together, but this relationship between two people, however deep at the time, needs to develop and mature with passing years. For that, it must be held in the web of family relationships, between parents and children, between grandparents and grandchildren, between cousins, aunts and uncles."

In addition to her relationship with the Duke of Edinburgh, the people closest to the Queen were her mother and her sister. For years, the Queen faithfully covered her mother's ongoing overdraft. Eventually, this, too, resulted in tabloid headlines in Britain. Although her more modest daughter could not understand the Queen Mother's extravagant lifestyle, she adored her

The Queen with Queen Elizabeth the Queen Mother and Princess Margaret posed for the Queen Mother's eightieth birthday.

Princess Elizabeth and Princess Margaret as children.

mother and faithfully called her twice a day on the telephone, no matter where she was in the world. Although an entirely different character, the Queen also loved her more complicated sister, Princess Margaret. In spite of the Queen having to tell Margaret that she could not retain her royal status if she married the divorced Group Captain Peter Townsend, and later having to give the Princess and her husband Lord Snowdon permission to divorce,

the sisters remained close until Princess Margaret's death in 2002, the Queen's Jubilee year.

According to Countess Mountbatten, "The Queen was wonderful with Princess Margaret's children when they had a difficult time and they spent a lot of time with her. And I imagine she's the same with her grandchildren."

The evidence seems to suggest that this is so. The Princess Royal's children, Peter and Zara Phillips, have a close, relaxed relationship with their royal grandparents. When they were very young, the Queen would visit them as often as she could, enjoying the informal country atmosphere at Gatcombe Park. In the immediate aftermath of Diana's death, Peter Phillips came to Balmoral at the Queen's request and was reportedly "a brick" while he helped to comfort the bereaved William and Harry. Zara Phillips is an independent young woman who, like her mother and grandmother, is a fine horsewoman. She has earned numerous

The Queen and the Duke with their then four grandchildren — Prince William, Prince Harry, Peter Phillips, and Zara Phillips.

awards for three-day eventing, including a world championship, and in 2006 she won the BBC's Sports Personality of the Year Award, as her mother did thirty-five years before.

The Princesses Beatrice and Eugenie of York also remain close to their Windsor grandparents. While the Duchess of York praises the Queen sincerely and often, Princess Eugenie gave her grandmother a more cutting-edge accolade, dubbing her "Super-Gran" on her MySpace page and listing the Queen as one of her heroes.

The Earl and Countess of Wessex (and presumably their daughter, Lady Louise) get on well with the Queen and Prince Philip. They have, after a few errors in judgement, become a dependable, hardworking couple who are particularly well received in Canada.

The Countess Mountbatten thinks that Super-Gran is "a very good description" of the Queen. In a piece in *Vanity Fair* magazine accompanying the official portraits taken of the Queen by American photographer Annie Leibovitz during her state visit to the United States in 2007, William Shawcross refers to Her Majesty's obvious devotion

Princesses Beatrice and Eugenie of York.

The Queen with her son and heir, the Prince of Wales.

to her seven grandchildren and her apparent eagerness to pick up their telephone calls, almost anytime and anywhere.

Naturally, Prince William and Prince Harry receive the most media attention among the Queen and the Duke's grandchildren. Now pursuing military careers, they garner extra attention from their grandparents as well, not only because of their places in the line of succession, but because of what they have already endured with the traumatic loss of their mother.

When the Queen and Duke were raising the Princes' father as Heir to the Throne, they made many errors in the eyes of the Prince of Wales. Instead of educating him at Buckingham Palace,

they sent Charles to day school at Hill House in London and to board at Cheam and finally Gordonstoun, the latter being a difficult place for him. Prince Philip explained his reason for sending his son to be educated in a classroom rather than by a governess at home: "We want him to go to school with other boys of his generation and to live with other children and absorb from childhood the discipline imposed by education with others." In the case of Gordonstoun, the Duke was merely following the tradition of fathers sending their sons to their old schools. However, when Philip attended Gordonstoun, it was a small, close school with instructors who were more like family than faculty. Over the years, the school grew and changed, and for all intents and purposes, Prince Charles attended a very different school than the one his father had experienced. At the time, it was argued that the Queen Mother thought Eton would be a more appropriate place for a future king to be educated. Whether or not this is true, both Prince William and Prince Harry attended school there and Prince William regularly spent Sunday afternoons with the Queen, discussing his future role as monarch. By letting Prince Philip take the lead in their children's education — by necessity — the Queen missed out on the chance to actively tutor the Prince of Wales in this way. Like most people, they are more relaxed and assured as grandparents than parents.

When asked about the Queen and Prince Philip's family life, Countess Mountbatten, herself a mother and grandmother, says,

> It must be difficult. They are a very, very close and very united and very loving couple and you know, are devoted to each other. They had four children and the children have the problems that all young people have these days and I can't imagine the difficulties of trying to deal with those problems in the public eye. It's bad enough as a private individual doing it privately, but in the public eye and everybody wanting to know what's

happened … terribly, really, really difficult. I think they've experienced much greater difficulties than the average couple in coping with growing up and coping with the disasters of the broken marriages.

Now that they are young men and have emerged from the protective mantle of school, William and Harry are subject to increasing press scrutiny. The Queen and the Duke have watched the second in line to the Throne and his brother make news in both their personal and professional lives. After much debate, Harry's deployment to Iraq was cancelled, a bitter experience for the young man whose life's dream — from a very young age — was to be a soldier. This situation is somewhat similar to his grandfather's stalled naval career, which was aborted because of the demands of his royal role. In Harry's case, it was not his welfare that was the deciding factor — after all, his uncle Prince Andrew served as a helicopter pilot during the Falklands War. Rather, it was the undue risk Harry's presence would place on his fellow soldiers under him.

Because of his university studies, William has not yet caught up to his younger brother militarily. However, the 2007 temporary breakup of his long-term relationship with Kate Middleton — whom he met at St. Andrew's University while they were both students there — put not only William but also the Queen on the front pages. Kate, a middle-class girl whose parents are self-made millionaires, behaved impeccably throughout the couple's courtship. While the young couple gave no reason for their separation, some factions of the press speculated that it was partly because the Queen supposedly found Kate's mother "common." Arthur Edwards, MBE and royal photographer for the British tabloid *The Sun* for more than thirty years, defended Her Majesty in print, writing that this snobbish and outdated attitude said more about royal commentators than it did the Queen, who would never be so small-minded. Her amicable relationship with the Countess of Wessex is proof that the Queen is not a rigid, inflexible monarch or mother-in-law.

Princes William and Harry joined their father, the Prince of Wales, on the slopes of Whistler, British Columbia, in March 1998.

Countess Mountbatten outlines the balancing act that royalty must perform: "The Queen and the Royal Family do not want to be in the forefront of fashion. On the other hand, you do want to gently move with the times and they've come a long way without being the leaders and without falling victim to fads.

"I think it's wonderful," she continues, "that they've been able to have such a good, stable marriage for sixty years, against all the odds in many cases. They've supported each other, loved each other and supported their families."

Prince Philip once said, "If you are really going to have a monarchy, you have got to have a family, and the family has got to be in the public eye." This is the challenge that must always be met by the Royal Family, if they are to survive as an institution. Like all parents, the Queen and the Duke of Edinburgh have admittedly made mistakes in raising their children. However, they have also given them an unequalled example of maintaining a marriage and a monarchy.

7
States, Travel, and Technology

"When you hear ... about the events in ... other places, ...
it is the Queen of Canada and her husband who are concerned in them"
— *Queen Elizabeth II*

The Queen's royal motto as Queen of Canada, *"A Mari Usque Ad Mare"* — "From Sea To Sea" — is taken from the 72nd Psalm, describing the King's dominion as being "from sea to sea and from the river unto the ends of the earth" — in other words as being universal. But while it is Her Majesty's Canadian motto it is not a bad description of the influence of the Queen and the Duke of Edinburgh in the world.

Sixteen states claim the Queen and Duke as their Sovereign and Consort — the United Kingdom of Great Britain and Northern Ireland, the Dominion of Canada, the Commonwealth of Australia, the Realm of New Zealand, Antigua and Barbuda, Bahamas, Barbados, Belize, Grenada, Jamaica, Papua New Guinea, Saint Christopher and Nevis,

Saint Lucia, Saint Vincent and the Grenadines, Solomon Islands, and Tuvalu. Another thirty-seven countries are members of the Commonwealth — this free association that encompasses one-third of the world's population, of which the Queen is Head and symbol. As a result, the Queen has many personae in the interaction of the states of the world and in the duties and travels she has undertaken, both on her own and with the Duke.

The international role of the Queen and the Duke is a complex and sophisticated one that has enriched their lives and the lives of their peoples around the world. But it is often not fully appreciated because too many people try to explain it, even if sympathetically, in the terms used by American republicanism, terms that cannot comprehend the nature of monarchical societies. The Queen

Because the Queen is the "State" the carriages in which she rides are called State carriages. In 2002 the Queen and the Duke of Edinburgh leave Buckingham Palace in the Gold State Coach for Golden Jubilee celebrations (above left). Close-up of the Gold State Coach (above right). The Australian State Coach was a gift to the Queen from the People of Australia (below left). Escorted by the Royal Canadian Mounted Police, the Queen arrives at Parliament Hill in the Canadian State Landau for Canada Day celebrations (below right).

is often described as the de jure "head of state" of a Commonwealth country while the Governor General is described as the de-facto "head of state" by people trying to explain the simple fact that the Queen has representatives because she cannot be everywhere at once, but succeeding only in causing unnecessary constitutional confusion.

In British or Canadian constitutional law there is no such thing as a "head of state," de jure or de facto. It is a republican term that is meaningless in a monarchy. The Queen is the legal embodiment of the State. That is to say, she *is* the State, not merely its head. This is actually quite a simple and logical concept, given the principles of common law. In British heritage countries the law deals only with individuals. A company, for example, exists in law as a corporate individual and is treated as an independent entity separate from its shareholders.

In the governmental structures of these countries the same principle applies. Municipalities are incorporated, so the people who live in a city are not themselves the city; the corporation is the city in each case. At the provincial and national levels of government, the government is not vested in an association of people but it is vested in a single legal individual — the Sovereign. The people live in the province or the country but they are not the province or the country in its legal persona: the Queen is. It is from this simple but fundamental principle that an understanding of the Queen and her Consort's roles in the world must begin.

Because the Queen is the State, everything of a public nature that she does, she does as the State. So she has but two natures — her private existence as a human being named Elizabeth and her public existence as one of her several states. The Duke of Edinburgh can act in three capacities. Like the Queen he has his personal life and he has a state role as Consort of the Queen, but, unlike the Queen, he can have a public life as an individual. Thus, for example, whenever the Queen comes to Canada, she does so as the Canadian State embodied and it is an official tour. There are no "private" tours of Canada by the Queen, though she may have private moments to herself on a tour. When the Duke of Edinburgh comes to Canada accompanying the Queen, he is part of that official tour, but he is also able to come on his own on an official tour as Consort or on a completely private tour, if he wishes. All three types of tours have taken place in Canada and throughout the Commonwealth and the world, and indeed even in locales within the United Kingdom.

And while the Queen is the State, she is in fact the embodiment of sixteen states simultaneously, and she always maintains all those roles regardless of which is being emphasized. While the Queen may delegate the exercise of her powers to her Governor General, she always remains the embodiment of the Canadian State no matter where she is in the world. And when she is in Canada, while her Canadian role may be paramount, she is still the embodiment of the British or the Australian State. On one occasion in Saudi Arabia, the Queen and Duke were on a state visit for Britain, but their Saudi hosts invited the ambassadors of all the Queen's realms to an official function, as a courtesy to the Queen's multinational status.

The Queen herself made this point emphatically early in her reign. In 1957, as she was leaving Canada for the United States, she told her Canadian people, "When you hear or read about the events in

Washington, and other places, I want you to reflect that it is the Queen of Canada and her husband who are concerned in them." She might as easily have made a similar speech about the Queen of New Zealand or the Bahamas when leaving those countries.

This transnational nature of the Queen's reign was evident from the beginning. It was not in England, on February 6, 1952, that Princess Elizabeth became Queen Elizabeth II, but in Kenya, on the first leg of what was intended to be a major Commonwealth tour of the Antipodes. That tour was rescheduled after the Coronation and began on November 23, 1953. Concluding on May 10, it was nearly six months in length and the itinerary included Canada (for a brief refuelling in Newfoundland of the royal airplane on the initial flight), Bermuda, Jamaica, Panama, Fiji, Tonga, New Zealand, Australia, Cocos Islands, Ceylon, Aden, Uganda, Libya, Malta, and Gibraltar. The royal couple travelled by airplane, ship, barge, horse-drawn carriage, rail, and numerous makes and models of automobiles. They had spent nearly one-quarter of the first twenty-seven months of the Queen's reign in lands other than the United Kingdom.

When the American President, George W. Bush, welcomed the Queen and the Duke of Edinburgh in 2007 to celebrate the founding of Jamestown, Virginia, he inadvertently started to refer to the Queen having been present in 1776 (the year of the American Declaration of Independence) instead of 1976 (for the two hundredth anniversary of the event). This led to considerable amusement and references to George Bush's propensity for verbal slips. However, he could almost be excused for the mistake. The Queen and Duke have been going to

The first American President to welcome the Queen to the United States was Harry Truman, who greeted the "Canadian Princess" in 1951.

The Queen and the American President Dwight Eisenhower view the St. Lawrence Seaway from the Britannia *in 1959, as the North American Monarch and President jointly opened the transportation corridor.*

the United States for so long that it probably seemed like they had been present at the founding. Their first visit was in 1951, before Elizabeth had become Queen. When they arrived from Canada, President Harry Truman greeted her as a "Canadian Princess," paying tribute to his northern neighbour. Although it does not constitute the whole of the history of the United States, as George Bush accidentally claimed, the fifty-six years that the Queen and Duke have been making American visits does constitute about one-quarter of that history. Truman, Eisenhower, Kennedy, Johnson, Nixon, Ford, Carter, Reagan, Bush, and Clinton are names of American presidents that even American schoolchildren may be forgetting but who were personal acquaintances of Elizabeth and Philip. And when Americans speak of "the Queen and the Duke" everyone knows which queen and duke they are referring to without further qualification.

But it is not just the Commonwealth and the Americans who have seen the royal couple so frequently or who give them a universal cachet. Virtually all of Europe, Africa, Asia, and Latin America have been visited by Elizabeth and Philip, and television has made them familiar faces to others who have not seen them in person. Their universal

The Queen was present at the bicentenary of the American Declaration of Independence in 1976 with the American President Gerald Ford, the Duke of Edinburgh, and Mrs. Ford.

appeal is so prevailing that countries frequently go to great lengths to emphasize personal ties. When Elizabeth and Philip visited Morocco in 1980, some British editorialists opined that Her Majesty would not be safe from Islamic extremists who were threatening the Muslim country. Moroccan officials replied that the Queen would be safe because she was a direct descendant of the Prophet Mohammed, so no Muslim could harm her. In 1984 the Queen and Duke went to China and the Chinese Government announced that their scholars had concluded the Queen was descended from the Tang Dynasty of Chinese Emperors.

The Queen and the Shōwa Emperor of Japan (Hirohito) share a toast during a state visit to Japan in 1975.

British observers also linked the Queen to great figures of their past. Following her accession numerous commentators and elements of the general populace drew connections between Queen Elizabeth II and her predecessor Queen Elizabeth I, with references to a new Elizabethan age. Mindful of the differences between herself and the Virgin Queen, and not wishing to have expectations placed on her to be someone other than herself, the Queen tried to diminish the imagery in her Christmas broadcast from New Zealand, stating, "I do not myself feel at all like my great Tudor forbear, who was blessed with neither husband nor children, who ruled as a despot and was never able to leave her native shores."

Similarly, Prince Philip wished to distance himself from close comparison to Prince Albert, who was not only his immediate predecessor as consort to a queen but was also his great-great-grandfather. While Prince Albert became Queen Victoria's official Private Secretary and was openly involved in meetings with ministers and state matters, Prince Philip shunned such a role and sought to carve out a niche for himself in non-state public life, while fully supporting the Queen as a husband in her public life. At the Queen's Coronation the Prince led the homage of the peers, swearing to be the Queen's "liege man of life and limb." He touched the Crown and kissed his Sovereign and wife on the cheek. It is an oath he has lived up to fully ever since, but he assumed no formal role as adviser in state affairs.

There were protocol matters to be resolved nonetheless. Initially, at the State Opening of Parliament the Queen sat on the Throne while the

At the Coronation of the Queen the Duke of Edinburgh kissed his Sovereign and wife when leading the peers in the homage ceremony.

Prince sat on a chair of estate to the side and one step below. This was a change from the position of Queen Consorts, who sat on a throne immediately next to their King's, and was seen, correctly, as a diminution of the status of the Duke. Similar seating arrangements were followed during the Commonwealth tour of 1953–54, when he sat on chairs to the side of and either below or slightly behind the Queen's Throne. This arrangement was changed within a few years, however, so that the Duke sits on a throne immediately beside Her Majesty when the Queen opens the British Parliament, as he also did in 1957 and 1977 when the Queen opened the Canadian Parliament.

On the 1953–54 tour of the Antipodes the Duke of Edinburgh sat on a chair to the side of and slightly behind the Throne when the Queen opened the New Zealand Parliament. In 1957, in Ottawa, the Duke, now Prince Philip, sat on a throne next to the Queen when she opened the Canadian Parliament.

In addition to accompanying the Queen on virtually all of her tours, the Duke of Edinburgh has travelled the world on behalf of projects of his own. He has undoubtedly been the Queen's second pair of eyes and ears in the world but he has made it clear his is not a second voice for the Queen. When he speaks, he speaks only for himself. And not being the embodiment of the State, as the Queen is, he is not bound by ministerial advice in expressing his views. Being forthright he has often ended up in hot

water in many lands, but he has always challenged his listeners to think.

The transnational travels of the Queen and the Duke of Edinburgh reflect the importance of the various parts of the world to them. As the United Kingdom is their senior realm, they reside in that country and spend the larger share of their time there. Canada is their second senior realm and it has appropriately seen the Queen and Duke more than any other land. It is truly their second home and in a

The Queen allowed her three sons to experience school in the three senior Commonwealth realms of Canada, Australia, and New Zealand. Prince Andrew attended Lakefield College, near Peterborough, in Canada in 1976 and 1977 and has returned to the Peterborough area on many occasions, including in 1985.

in a more personal decision — the schooling of their children. Each of their three sons was sent to experience school in one of the senior monarchies. The Prince of Wales attended Timbertops School in Australia in 1966, Prince Andrew spent two terms at Lakefield College in Canada in 1976–77, and Prince Edward went to Collegiate School Wanganui in New Zealand in 1982.

When the Queen and Duke flew to Gander, Newfoundland, on November 23, 1953, to start their six-month Commonwealth tour, it was the first time that a monarch had flown across the Atlantic. Air travel would make the world a smaller place in the Queen's reign for everyone, not least the Queen herself. The Queen and Prince Philip could travel from London to Ottawa faster than Queen Victoria and Prince Albert could travel to Scotland. It was air travel that made a shared, worldwide monarchy a reality as well as a political principle.

But while air travel was critical to the new-style monarchy, a more traditional mode of transportation remained at centre stage. The international duties of the royal couple, their relationship as spouses, and their public and personal interests came together and were almost perfectly symbolized in the Royal Yacht *Britannia*. The *Britannia* replaced the *Victoria and Albert III*, which was completed in 1901 and had followed the *Victoria and Albert I*, launched in 1842, and the *Victoria and Albert II*, which replaced the first in 1855. The three *Victoria and Albert*s were used for international travel but that was limited to the English Channel and North Sea and the Mediterranean. When King George VI announced in October 1951 that there would be a new yacht, he intended it for worldwide travel to service the

category of its own. Australia, New Zealand, and the other Commonwealth realms over which the Queen is Sovereign are next in receiving the royal couple's presence. They, in turn, are followed by the other countries in the Commonwealth, by the United States, and by the rest of the world.

The importance of the Commonwealth realms was also made clear by the Queen and the Duke new Commonwealth of independent monarchies of which he was Sovereign.

The *Britannia* was launched on April 16, 1953, the year of the Queen's Coronation, and commissioned on January 7, 1954. This was after the Queen and the Duke had left for their first Commonwealth tour, so its service began when it met them in Libya on the return to Britain, bringing Prince Charles and Princess Anne to meet their parents.

As part of King George VI's other requirement, that the yacht be economical, it was constructed so that it could be converted into a hospital ship in time of war, with the royal apartments being convertible to hospital wards for two hundred patients. It was a well-meaning concept, but the ship was never so used, and the fact that it had always

The Britannia *became an icon throughout the Commonwealth as it served as the home of the Queen and the Duke of Edinburgh in many lands. A commemorative plate marking the opening of the St. Lawrence Seaway featured the* Britannia.

been claimed it would be actually caused negative controversy in 1982 during the Falklands War when the Admiralty decided it was too valuable to risk in the South Atlantic in such a capacity. This provided fuel to those who wished to scrap the ship as a royal extravagance.

As the King had died before the keel was laid, it was Queen Elizabeth II and the Duke of Edinburgh who oversaw the construction. They took a personal interest in the building and insisted on simpler designs for the royal apartments, which they thought were too fancy in the original plans. Furnishings from the *Victoria and Albert* were used where practical to save money and to preserve an element of tradition and continuity from the old yacht to the new. For its more demanding international future it was fitted with stabilizers and air conditioning. For entertaining, the reception rooms could accommodate 250 guests. A Royal Marines band was embarked for entertainment and ceremonial purposes. It was a simple palace at sea but a palace nonetheless.

Although it was a British ship, paid for by the British Government and manned by sailors from the Royal Navy, it became an icon of the Commonwealth. It travelled to Canada a dozen times in its life, and images of it on the Atlantic or Pacific coasts or negotiating the St. Lawrence Seaway and the Great Lakes, with the Queen and her Consort and other members of the Royal Family on the bridge, are as much a part of Canadian folklore as are images of it in the Solent to British memory.

For the Queen and the Duke it combined their Commonwealth responsibilities with their personal love of the sea, and Philip was back in his element as

The Britannia *flew the royal banner and the national flag of whatever country in the Queen's realm she was in. Here, in Canadian waters, she flew the Queen's royal banner for Canada from the main mast and the Canadian national flag from the mizzen-mast.*

a naval officer. The usual procedure on royal tours was not for the royal couple to sail to the distant destination on the *Britannia* but for the yacht to sail in advance of the tour to the starting place of the cruise, to be met there by the royals who arrived by airplane. When sailing in the waters of a Commonwealth country of which the Queen was Sovereign, the Queen's royal banner for the realm concerned would be flown from the main mast, the national flag of the country from the mizzen-mast,

and the Admiralty flag from the foremast. The Royal Union Flag flew from the jackstaff and the White Ensign from the stern.

On December 11, 1997, the Royal Yacht *Britannia* was decommissioned after sailing for forty-four years and over a million nautical miles. She was not replaced. The *Britannia* had been a symbol of Commonwealth identity as she sailed to all parts of the worldwide family, providing the only common home for their Queen shared by

In 1976 the Britannia *was the site for a dinner given by the Queen and the Duke for the Queen's representatives and first ministers of Canada.*

the various countries. She had sailed the Atlantic and the Pacific, the Mediterranean and the Baltic. She had traversed the Great Lakes of Canada and the warm waters of Australia and New Zealand. Air travel made her unnecessary, perhaps, but her end was a sad moment.

Its importance to the Commonwealth might have been more evident if its crew had been drawn from the navies of all the Commonwealth realms or if the Commonwealth governments had contributed to the cost of maintaining her, but a piece of the fabric that holds the Commonwealth together was unravelled when the *Britannia* sailed no more. Ironically she was decommissioned on the anniversary of the Statute of Westminster, which recognized the equality of all the Sovereign's realms and created the Commonwealth.

The waves of the sea and the air carried the Queen and Prince Philip to their many realms and beyond but it was airwaves of a new kind that transformed their ability to communicate with the Queen's peoples in a different way.

As Prince of Wales, King Edward VIII was the first member of the Royal Family to give an address using the new invention of the wireless on October 7, 1922, to fifty thousand Boy Scouts. The first reigning monarch to use the communications tool was King George V on April 23, 1924, when he opened the Empire Exhibition at Wembley. With his first Christmas message to the Empire on Christmas Day 1932 he took the technology to a new level and inspired the American President, Franklin Roosevelt, who modelled his famous radio "fireside chats" with Americans on the King's technique.

Queen Elizabeth II first broadcast to the Empire during the Second World War, but it was her 1947 broadcast from South Africa, on her coming of age, when she pledged a life of service to the Commonwealth, that remains in the historic memory of her peoples as the great event.

Television found the Royal Family quite early in its infancy. The opening of the Olympic Games at Wembley by King George VI on July 29, 1948, was the first televised royal event. Princess Elizabeth first appeared in television coverage on April 30, 1951, and on October 10 of that year the television cameras were at Heathrow as the Princess and the Duke of Edinburgh boarded their aircraft to fly to Canada for an extensive cross-country tour. It was the first of a lifetime of such airport scenes captured by television. King George VI's funeral in 1952 and the Queen's Coronation in 1953 were the first great state ceremonies to be televised to the world, though the film was flown across the Atlantic to be rebroadcast in Canada and the United States, not transmitted live as such an event would be in the twenty-first-century world of twenty-four-hour television news.

In 1947 Princess Elizabeth broadcast to the peoples of the Commonwealth from South Africa by radio to mark her twenty-first birthday (left). In 1957, as Queen, she made her first television address from Ottawa, the Canadian capital (right).

In 1957 the Queen was in Ottawa to open the Canadian Parliament on Monday, October 14, which was also the Canadian Thanksgiving holiday. It was the occasion for another royal landmark, as Her Majesty broadcast to Canadians on the Sunday eve of the holiday in the first live television broadcast by a monarch. It was a prelude to the 1957 Christmas message, which would be broadcast by television as well as by radio that year. But not only was the Queen coming into the homes of her people via television, the people were soon to be let into her homes via the same medium.

In 1969 the landmark television show *The Royal Family* was presented. It was seen as an opportunity to use that medium to reach a new generation who were growing up in a television world. Not only were members of the Royal Family seen performing their public duties but aspects of their private lives were viewed as well. It was controversial at the time, although it seems tame from the twenty-first-century perspective of reality television, the Internet, YouTube, and cellphone cameras recording intimate details of personal lives for the world to see that but a generation ago would not have interested even the

In a scene from the television documentary The Royal Family *in 1969, the Queen points to Australia on a globe of the world, reflecting her worldwide sovereignty and activities.*

presenter's own relatives but are now devoured by an undiscriminating public.

To some it was a dynamic and positive innovation for the Royal Family. To others it was letting too much daylight in upon the magic. And to extreme pessimists it was not letting daylight in but darkness, like the vampire of legend who could only enter a dwelling if invited, but then drained the life from its hosts. Forty years on there is still evidence to support in some degree each of these assessments. It brought a massive new reach for monarchy to spread its benefits in the world, but it also provided the means for self-destruction for members of the Royal Family if they were not careful. But the initiative had the support of the Queen and the Duke at the time, and the world could not be turned back afterwards. Television, and in the current century the Internet, had to be faced and mastered. It could not have been ignored.

At her coming-of-age birthday on April 21, 1947, the same year she would be married, Princess Elizabeth addressed the Commonwealth:

> I declare before you all that my whole life, whether it be long or short, shall be devoted to your service and the service of our great imperial Commonwealth to which we all belong. But I shall not have strength to carry out this resolution unless you join in it with me, as I now invite you to do; I know that your support will be unfailingly given. God bless all of you who are willing to share it.

The Queen has said that the Duke of Edinburgh is owed by many countries "a debt greater than he would ever claim."

The Duke of Edinburgh, who became her husband seven months later, has led the Queen's peoples in providing that support. At their golden wedding anniversary luncheon at the Banqueting Hall in Whitehall on November 20, 1997, the Queen said of her Consort, "He is someone who doesn't take easily to compliments but he has, quite simply, been my strength and stay all these years, and I, and his whole family, and this and many other countries, owe him a debt greater than he would ever claim, or we shall ever know."

The international appeal of Queen Elizabeth II and the Duke of Edinburgh is due not only to who

The Queen, the Duke of Edinburgh, Queen Elizabeth the Queen Mother, the Prince of Wales, the Princess Royal, and the Commonwealth heads of government at the 1997 Commonwealth meeting in Edinburgh.

they are, though that is undoubtedly significant, but to what they have done with who they are. They have become consummate professionals in their vocation, in their own Commonwealth lands and as representatives of those lands to the wider world. Walter Bagehot, the nineteenth-century political theorist, said that the Monarch has "the right to be consulted, the right to encourage and the right to warn." The Queen and the Duke's intimate knowledge of and respect for the people, institutions, and identity of the many countries in the Commonwealth make their advice a welcome asset for political and community leaders when it is sought out and offered. The royal couple's experience in international relations is appreciated by the peoples of other lands. The Queen, the Duke, and the peoples of their realms, of their Commonwealth, and, indeed, of the world have created an international circle of reciprocal service and support over sixty years unknown to history in its depth, breadth, and vitality, from sea to sea and from the river unto the ends of the earth.

Riding the Contentious Kingdom

"I feel proud and happy to be the Queen of such a nation"
— *Elizabeth II, Ottawa, 1957, making the first TV broadcast of her life*

On Easter Monday, April 9, 2007, Her Majesty Queen Elizabeth II, Queen of Canada, and His Royal Highness The Prince Philip, Duke of Edinburgh, arrived at Vimy in northern France. It was a memorial service of poignant national significance that brought the royal couple to the former battlefield of the Great War on the Douai Plain. The lightly cloudy day was rife with the scent and softness of spring; the Vimy Memorial, newly cleansed of dirt, the decay of sixty-one years repaired, towered pristinely on the ridge. Excited by the royal couple's arrival, a crowd of veterans, officials, four thousand high school students, military and RCMP, people from near and far — twenty thousand in all — forgot for a moment the damper that news of the deaths of six Canadian soldiers from a roadside bomb in Afghanistan the day before had put on this, the commemoration of the ninetieth anniversary of the Battle of Vimy Ridge.

Greeted by her eleventh and newest Canadian Prime Minister, Stephen Harper, and the French Prime Minister, Dominique de Villepin, the Queen received the royal salute and reviewed a guard of honour. In 1922 the Vimy site was given by France to Canada but remains under French sovereignty. When her uncle King Edward VIII as King of Canada first dedicated the memorial seventy-one years before, he was there first to receive the French President, Albert Lebrun. This time the French representative was the Prime Minister, not the head of state, so the Queen as Canada's Sovereign arrived last.

Her Majesty mounted the platform with Prince Philip for the ceremony. In her speech, she called the capture of Vimy Ridge in 1917, in which 3,598 Canadian soldiers were killed and 7,000 wounded, a "stunning victory" that altered the course of the First World War. Canadians finally took the ridge after two years of unsuccessful attempts by British and

Beginning a walkabout following rededication of the Vimy Monument, April 9, 2007, the Queen is accompanied by the Duke of Edinburgh, Colonel-in-Chief of The Royal Canadian Regiment, and followed by the Prime Minister, Rt. Hon. Stephen Harper.

French forces. In the process Canadian nationhood was tested, triumphed, and gained new strength and purpose. By their victory Canadian soldiers, the Queen said, turned the battlefield "from a symbol of despair into a source of inspiration." She concluded: "To those who have so recently lost their lives in Afghanistan, to Canada and to all who serve the cause of freedom, I rededicate this magnificently restored memorial."

The Queen accepted a bouquet from Rachel Harper, six-year-old daughter of the Prime Minister, and with the Duke of Edinburgh went on a walkabout, the royal couple following their usual practice of separating to talk to as many people as possible. The 2007 Vimy rededication ceremony was another class act performance by the almost eighty-one-year-old monarch, supported by her husband of nearly sixty years, and their presence enhanced

On a podium draped with the Canadian Red Ensign, King Edward VIII, uncle of Queen Elizabeth II, as Monarch of Canada conducts the original dedication of the Vimy Memorial, 1936.

the event in a way nothing else could. It was entirely fitting that the Queen of Canada preside at this historic occasion so symbolic of Canada and it was a triumph for Elizabeth II personally, though in characteristic fashion she gave no sign of that. Not for years had her government in Ottawa asked Her Majesty to act as Queen of Canada in an international setting. Her eager compliance with

The ongoing commitment: arrival of the Queen of Canada and the Duke of Edinburgh at Vimy Ridge, 2007.

their request showed how keenly after fifty-five years she still valued and was bent upon fulfilling her role as the Canadian Sovereign.

To observers, the Queen at Vimy was a potent reminder that from the time of her marriage in 1947 Canada was the country to which she and Philip had given more of themselves than any other part of the Commonwealth apart from the United Kingdom. It is in regard to Canada also that the functioning of the partnership of Elizabeth and Philip in their public life and its positive impact can most clearly be seen. Years before, in October 1951, when Princess Elizabeth disembarked from her transatlantic flight and first set foot on the soil of Canada, it seemed to Canadians that it had taken a long time to get her to the country. Thwarted was the chance of her spending part of her childhood in the Dominion when her father was unable to accept the position of Governor General in 1930; vain the publicly expressed hope that she would accompany her parents on the great royal tour of 1939; unrealized the wish to provide a safe haven for her in Canada during the Blitz. But wartime contacts of Canadians with their princess intensified the longing to have her among them. As it happened, Philip arrived ahead of her in 1941 as a midshipman in the *Valiant* escorting Canadian troops to Europe to fight Hitler. But when Princess Elizabeth and her husband of not quite four years finally did come, it was the people who brought them. Invitations poured into Ottawa from Canadians in all walks of life, though the Government seemed reluctant to agree even when the Princess did until it could no longer ignore requests from the three Canadian units whose Colonel-in-Chief she was.

Once Ottawa got on the bandwagon, Elizabeth and Philip found their envisaged fortnight holiday trip in Canada turned into a six-week tour across the country and back, with a brief visit to the United States where Elizabeth was to appear as "the Canadian Princess." That was Her Majesty's introduction to Canada. It was her first big solo tour, "the final stages in the education of a princess," as one journalist put it, and because of delays caused by the King's health it took place in the autumn, not the ideal time for journeys in Canada. Just the same, striking vignettes of this meeting of the future Queen and the mass of Canadians abide: Philip and Elizabeth square dancing at Rideau Hall, the royal couple wrapped up in blankets at the Calgary Stampede, their sleigh ride in the falling snow at St. Agathe in the Laurentians. People, it was said, watched the Princess closely to see if she measured up to the royal tradition. Evidently they were satisfied, as was the Princess herself, and at the end she told them, "We have been welcomed with a warmth of heart that has made us feel how truly we belong to Canada."

When the King died, Canada was the first Commonwealth country to proclaim Elizabeth II "Queen" and "Supreme Liege Lady in and over Canada," ahead of Britain even, and Canadians mourned the beloved George VI and bought a novelty called television to watch the Coronation festivities of his daughter. Prince Philip by 1951 had sacrificed his naval career to his role as royal consort and carefully thought out what his line of action should be as the Queen's husband. His function, he concluded, was to be a serious support, both public and private, to his wife, but not to be involved in constitutional or political matters. Moreover

Treasured moments from the first tour: Elizabeth and Philip square dance at Rideau Hall; snowflakes dot the Princess's coat as she and the Duke, wearing Western headgear, watch a specially restaged Calgary Stampede.

he resolved never to play up the phenomenal popularity he and the Queen enjoyed as the reign began. "I took a conscious decision not to do that," he told Gyles Brandreth, author of *Elizabeth and Philip: Portrait of a Royal Marriage*, years later.

During the first Canadian tour he conducted

Souvenirs of the 1951 tour.

himself according to plan, always present in the background, lending a hand when something went wrong, relieving awkwardness with a flash of wit or trenchant word. After the Coronation and subsequent world tour Philip showed how he would support the Queen in Canada between times. In August 1954 he made a solo trip through the country in which he saw a lot of the North as well as the scientific and industrial work Canadians were doing. The knowledge and feel for things thus acquired by the Duke of Edinburgh, the identification of problems in a way that transcended solutions limited by the narrowness of a political line, were an obvious help to his wife, and by taking an interest in the lives of Canadians as the Queen's husband he made her a reality to them. More mundane royal duties were included, of course: opening buildings, presenting colours, making speeches. In this way

Philip began to leave his own mark on Canada, whether by challenging long-standing but unhelpful myths such as that Canada "was a young country" (1951), telling Canadians they were physically out of shape and should do something about it (1959), or urging Ontario politicians to update their obsolete liquor laws (1959).

For Elizabeth and Philip the 1950s was a decade of orientation, education, and growth in Canada. Both major political parties were united in their support of the Crown: the Liberals under the cautious Louis St. Laurent arranged the Queen's historic opening of Parliament in Ottawa, and the Conservatives, who unexpectedly came to power under the populist John Diefenbaker, carried it out in 1957. The Queen was the centre of that colourful, busy Thanksgiving weekend in Ottawa, a faultless performer in the magnificent pageant in her High

June 1953 scout magazine's iconic Queen conveys the Canadian Coronation mood of jubilation and awe.

Inuit meet Philip on his 1954 solo fact-finding tour of the Canadian North.

Court of Parliament, showing Canadians could stage ceremony without circus, pomp without pomposity. "I greet you as your Queen. Together we constitute the Parliament of Canada," she declared to the assembled Senators, MPs, diplomats, Canadian Forces personnel, and wives in the Senate chamber and to Canadians across the land. A somewhat nervous Elizabeth also made the first TV broadcast of her life and, with Philip looking on, modestly accepted critical coaching from the local producer that shocked her entourage.

Canada was still at one with the vision the Fathers of Confederation had of the country as monarchical America in contrast to republican America south of the border. Canada's status as a separate monarchy in the 1931 Statute of Westminster was not fully implemented, and the attractive young Sovereign and her capable consort were an incentive to get on with it. Parliament assented to the Queen's title "Queen of Canada" in 1953 and Canada was mentioned specifically in the Coronation Oath; the Canadian Guards were set up to stress the Monarch's separate Canadian role the same year; Philip was made a member of the Queen's Privy Council for

The Queen receives the royal salute as she arrives on Parliament Hill with the Duke of Edinburgh to become the first Monarch to open her Canadian Parliament in person, October 14, 1957. For this occasion Her Majesty wore her magnificent Coronation dress with its design of maple leaves and other Commonwealth emblems.

COMMEMORATING EVENTS OF
GREAT SIGNIFICANCE TO THE PEOPLE OF

ONTARIO

The Opening of the St. Lawrence Seaway

1959

*and the visit of H. M. Queen Elizabeth II
and
H. R. H. The Prince Philip, Duke of Edinburgh*

JUNE — JULY, 1959

Police have difficulty holding back enthusiastic Montreal crowds on 1959 royal tour (above). Programme for opening of the St. Lawrence Seaway 1959 (right).

Canada in 1957; the Queen personally announced the appointment of the new Governor General in Halifax at the end of the 1959 tour; and Her Majesty adopted a personal banner based on the Canadian Royal Arms in 1962. Most Canadians were pleased with this boost to their sense of identity, which had already been enhanced by the experience of the war and the growth and achievements since. The Queen regretted that the Prince of Wales could not go to school or university in Canada, as had been urged; the media she felt would never leave him alone.

Expanded and improved air travel rendered the great coast-to-coast and back royal tours obsolete and the decade ended with the last of them, an exhausting journey of forty-five thousand miles in forty-five days. It celebrated the decade's major

Canadian achievement, the opening of the St. Lawrence Seaway at Cornwall on June 26, 1959, carried out jointly by the Queen of Canada and the President of the United States. Aboard *Britannia* the royal couple sailed through the seaway inland to Port Arthur at the western end of Lake Superior. Towards the end of the tour Canadians were disturbed by the unusual spectacle of the Queen cancelling engagements because of fatigue. In fact, as they soon learned, she was pregnant with Prince Andrew but had told no one except her Canadian Prime Minister.

This promising opening of the reign ended

with the events of 1964. If the Queen was surprised by the upsurge of separatism and the explosion of the quiet revolution that greeted her and the Duke of Edinburgh when they reached Quebec City, after marking the centenary of the Charlottetown Conference in Prince Edward Island in October of that year, so was Quebec's Premier, Jean Lesage. So moved was Lesage by Elizabeth's serenity, majesty, and courage in the face of separatist violence and insults, he kept bursting into tears. The jarring incident, however, was not really a clash between Queen and people but between police and a gang of youths who rushed police headquarters demanding the release of a well-known separatist, Reggie Chartrand. It was the threat of violence that kept people off the streets. The Prime Minister, Lester Pearson, was also present and recorded that the Queen, whom he described as "far more calm than her husband," took it philosophically, even expressing amusement when students showing her their backs could not resist twisting their heads "to see what I looked like."

Ironically, as the separatists demonstrated outside, the Queen in the Quebec Legislature was defending French-Canadian culture. "It is agreeable to me to think that there exists in our Commonwealth a country where I can express myself officially in French," she said. Separatists reviled the Queen because she symbolized Canadian unity, but Her Majesty in the long run, instead of being hailed for championing her country, was unjustly labelled by some federalists as responsible for the turmoil.

A segment of public opinion, small and mainly English-speaking but increasingly vociferous, claimed the Crown was the problem in Canada and should be superseded. Did it not occur to them that the growth of nationalism in English Canada helped reanimate French-Canadian nationalism for which Quebec not Canada was "the nation"? Their solution was to replace the Crown with symbols of what they called Canadian nationalism — a flag, anthem, and the myth of a struggle for Canadian independence and identity. Canadians should hate their history. The idea of sharing a monarch with other countries, though Canada had always done it, suddenly became repugnant. This position ignored an important fact: Canada was put together on the basis of allegiance, not race, blood, or language. The flag debate was underway at this time, and Elizabeth and Philip had laughed over the more absurd manifestations of the controversy unexpectedly encountered during their tour. Choosing a flag, however, was not a repudiation of the Crown.

By the 1960s a more nationalistic mood characterized English Canadians, a nationalism very American in nature but not openly hostile to monarchy. English-Canadian nationalism came partly from the inundation of Canadian culture by Americanism and the superficial comparisons it led to. Another ingredient in the unsettled 1960s, a decade of ideologies, was the spread of the Marxist analysis of man, history, and economics in Canadian universities and schools. In such a climate authority, particularly monarchy, could expect to be discounted. The events of 1964 gave the enemies of the Crown, and there had always been critics, what they were looking for — a pretext for hostility to the Queen. From that time at the official level bias against the Queen and her family became institutionalized.

The first negative result of 1964 was a curtailed role for the Queen and Duke in the

Whether opening Parliament (as in 1977, above left), receiving civic welcomes (Toronto, 1959, below), or holding an investiture of the Order of Canada (Ottawa, 1973, above right), the Queen has given countless Canadian celebrations glamour, colour, and simple dignity.

gigantic nationwide celebration of the hundredth anniversary of Confederation three years later. Though the Queen presided on July 1 on Parliament Hill in Ottawa and made her brief visit to Expo '67 in Montreal where she rode on the minirail, there were no visits by the Sovereign to other parts of Canada that such an important year ought to have seen. When the Order of Canada was established in the year of the country's centenary, the Queen was, it is true, its Sovereign, but appointments were to be made by the Governor General and only approved by Her Majesty. It took little time for the future of the Crown to be discussed at the highest levels. According to *Mike*, Lester Pearson's memoirs, the Queen's concern about national unity caused her to raise the question of the future of the Monarchy during an audience the retiring Prime Minister had

with her at Buckingham Palace. Or was it the Prime Minister who asked that it be brought up?

The climate might be changing but Philip continued quietly supporting his wife according to plan. Pearson paid tribute to the Duke's "great help" in the "relaxing process" on the 1964 tour. In a 1966 speech in Scarborough, Ontario, His Royal Highness pointed out how there was a difference between patriotism and narrow nationalism; the presence of the Royal Family, he said, encouraged the former.

After marking the Centennial year with the Queen, the Duke returned a few weeks later to open

The Duke of Edinburgh continued his support of the Queen of Canada with his own full and varied programme. In 1962 His Royal Highness laid the cornerstone of Massey College in Toronto (above) and in 2002 returned to mark the college's fortieth anniversary and become an Honorary Senior Fellow. Duke of Edinburgh's Award media portfolio from the 1980s (right).

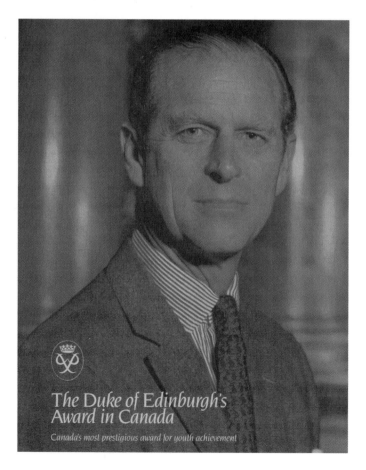

The Duke of Edinburgh's
Award in Canada

Canada's most prestigious award for youth achievement

the Pan American Games in Winnipeg. The Queen's husband had in 1963 introduced his Duke of Edinburgh's Award Scheme in Canada to help solve the problems of youth in the fourteen to twenty-one age bracket. Also early in this decade the second Duke of Edinburgh's Commonwealth Study Conference was held in Canada. This idea came out of Philip's concern for the consequences of industrialization, and brought together people from corporations, trade unions, public administration bodies, and universities to influence young leaders, so that when they were in positions of authority they could make decisions with some knowledge of their consequences. The Study Conferences continue today.

Philip was a pioneer in another way. As early as 1967 he told Canadians to be concerned about the environment. "Conservation … is really a case of now or never," he said to the Canadian Audubon Society that year. "If we don't get it right now, there won't be a second chance." In the final year of the 1960s, the Duke made a fifteen-day tour of eleven Canadian cities. The same year found him explaining the reason for separatism and the unique character of Quebec on NBC television and radio in Washington.

The 1970s witnessed the crucial institutional battle for the Monarchy. For most Canadians the Crown remained a given: Elizabeth and Philip were popular and monarchy was useful to Canada, something the country was reminded of by the royal couple's 1970 tour of the Northwest Territories. The Trudeau Cabinet might downplay the notion, but one purpose of the Queen's tour of the North was to let the United States and the world know its sovereignty belonged to Canada. Did the country have anyone who was a bigger draw for the global media than its Queen? The Queen was useful too when it came to the Native peoples, learning as they were to voice the very real injustices they suffered. When she flew to Manitoba for its centenary following the Northwest Territories tour, the chief at the Pas Indian Reserve publicly begged Her Majesty to get the Government to help his people. In 1970 the Queen played a

On the 1970 tour of the Northwest Territories and Manitoba, the Queen began introducing her children to Canada. Duke of Edinburgh with Princess Anne (now Princess Royal) in the fur shop at Inuvik.

card of her own to strengthen the Crown: her family. Canadians in the North and Manitoba were delighted to get to know the young Prince of Wales and his sister, Princess Anne, who accompanied their parents. It was the first of the family tours.

Canadians saw a lot of the Queen and her husband in the 1970s. It helped that a number of provincial centenaries came up: Manitoba in 1970, British Columbia in 1971, and Prince Edward Island in 1973. Her Majesty and His Royal Highness presided at them all, the Queen joking that Canada must soon run out of centenaries. In Toronto in 1973 Elizabeth made a much-quoted speech addressing her role in the rapidly expanding multicultural character of Canadian society: "I want the Crown to be seen as a symbol of national sovereignty belonging to all … a link … between Canadian citizens of every national origin and ancestry." When the Commonwealth Conference was held in Ottawa in August, Elizabeth returned for it, making clear that she was receiving the Commonwealth Heads of Government at Rideau Hall as Queen of Canada, the host country, as well as Head of the Commonwealth. The conference being political and constitutional, Philip was present but had his own programme. The Queen's media coup of the decade, however, came after she opened the XXI Olympic Games in Montreal in July 1976 and, as a proud and radiant mother, assembled the whole of her immediate family at Bromont, Quebec, a first for Canada.

During the summer of 1978, Elizabeth and Philip brought their younger sons, Prince Andrew and Prince Edward, when they toured the Maritimes prior to Her Majesty opening the XI Commonwealth Games in Edmonton. No one doubted the Queen

when she said at the provincial dinner, "I am getting to know our country rather well." In the 1970s too she changed her mind about the feasibility of her children getting some of their education in Canada and, in a highly popular move, allowed her second son, Prince Andrew, to spend two terms at Lakefield College in Ontario. On a solo engagement in October 1978 Philip was presented with the Award of the St. Boniface Hospital Research Centre for his promotion of physical fitness. It is one of the few acknowledgements he has ever received for his contributions to Canadian life. Since 1976 he had been involved in planning for his Fifth Commonwealth Study Conference, scheduled to take place in Kingston and Calgary in 1980.

The Queen had celebrated the Silver Jubilee of her reign in Ottawa in October 1977. She again opened Parliament, Philip at her side, in a scene of brilliant mediaeval pageantry and serious contemporary significance. "I dedicate myself anew to the people I am proud to serve," she declared with customary convincing sincerity to Members of Parliament, many of whom ironically were even then working to remove her.

In the thirteen years since the 1964 tour, the Queen's policy on the Crown had remained firm and clear. In public she maintained her constitutional non-partisanship and made no mention of possible changes or debates on the future of her Throne. In private, she exercised her "right to warn," her privilege of challenging the wisdom of her government's policy and actions, arguing with her Prime Minister over government measures and attempting to talk the Ministry into changing them, even if unsuccessfully. This she did in 1972 when Trudeau stripped her of one of the basic rights of sovereignty — issuing the letters of credence and recall of Canadian ambassadors. The Queen lost and the functions passed to the Governor General, but the record was clear to history that she did her duty in opposing an underhanded, unnecessary alteration of standard constitutional practice.

"It is … a misconception to believe that the Monarchy exists in the interests of the Monarch. It exists solely in the interests of the people," Prince Philip told the parliamentary press corps in a much publicized news conference in Ottawa at the end of 1969. The brutally frank remarks of the off-the-cuff spokesman of "the firm" could be taken as the Queen's view too. The royal couple knew the Crown was in crisis.

Discontent over the government's elimination of royal symbols, reduction of the Canadian Guards, abolition of salutes on anniversaries such as the Coronation, and turning Royal Mail into Canada Post beginning that year, however, showed the Crown's foes that they were unlikely to gain a clear majority in any vote on abolishing the Queen. Pierre Trudeau, Her Majesty's fourth Prime Minister, though he came to like and respect the Queen as a person, was no lover of monarchy. A twofold strategy emanated from him: appease royalist Canadians by lots of visits by the Queen and her family; at the

Cartoonist's view of the Premiers' reaction to the Trudeau Government's attempt to eliminate the Queen in 1979.

same time divest the Queen of the exercise of her functions bit by bit and transfer them to the Governor General. The second part could be done behind the scenes without formal constitutional change and thus little public fallout. After 1973 the Queen no longer held investitures of the Order of Canada, for example. Her Majesty must have mused on how the Canadian electorate was never asked if this is what it wanted and also have noticed that the constitutional position of the Governor General vis-à-vis the Prime Minister was actually weakened in the process, as a viceroy dissociated from the Queen was easier to ignore.

It was in June 1978, barely half a year after the Queen's happy Silver Jubilee, that Elizabeth and Philip found themselves faced with a major constitutional threat to the position of the Sovereign in Canada, the gravest of the reign. It took the form of the Constitutional Amendment Bill, Bill C-60, introduced by the Trudeau Cabinet. The Bill left no doubt that transferring the exercise of the Queen's functions to the Governor General was only preparation for more far-reaching changes. The Bill proposed removal of the Queen as part of Parliament, abolition of her Prerogative Power, the vesting of authority in the Governor General instead of the Queen, conversion of the Queen's Privy Council for Canada into a Council of State, and the termination of the Queen's right to appoint her personal representative, who instead would be not only nominated but also appointed by the government of the day. If and when she was in Canada, the Queen might be allowed to exercise the *Governor General's* powers. Had it been accepted as it stood, Bill C-60 would have created a Gilbert and Sullivan fantasy scenario for Canada.

Elizabeth could not speak out in defence of her own role without abandoning the Crown's well-

Metal pin commemorating proclamation of the revised Canadian Constitution by Queen Elizabeth II in 1982.

established non-partisanship. Nor could Philip enter the debate more than he already had. The Queen's interests as Sovereign were at odds with the legislative projects of her appointed government. It was a very tricky situation requiring the most skilful handling by the Monarch. Who if anyone would defend the Queen? Champions appeared: the Premiers of the ten Canadian provinces, including René Lévesque's separatist government in Quebec. In an August 10, 1978, communiqué the Premiers rejected vesting authority in a federal government appointee rather than the customary hereditary monarch. They explained why, adding a telling definition to Canadian constitutional parlance: "the system of democratic parliamentary government requires an ultimate authority to ensure its responsible nature and to safeguard against abuses of power. That ultimate power must not be an instrument of the federal Cabinet. The Premiers, therefore, oppose constitutional changes that substitute for the Queen as ultimate authority, a Governor General whose appointment and dismissal would be solely at the pleasure of the federal Cabinet." Ironically, but appropriately, the Prime Minister announced the demise of Bill C-60 on February 6, 1979 — the anniversary of the Queen's accession to Canada's Throne. It was a vindication of Her Majesty's twenty-five years of service as Queen as much as of a system of government.

Had she been the kind of person to think that way, Elizabeth II could have enjoyed a rueful laugh at the fact that when the new constitutional settlement was concluded, she herself rescued the inauguration ceremony from being a non-event. For, abandoning the idea of emasculating the Monarchy, the Trudeau

Cabinet had moved on to the more emotionally charged and more promising vote-catcher issue of patriation and the Charter of Rights and Freedoms, and a settlement was achieved, though one that for the first time was forced on Quebec, a circumstance that saddened the Queen.

Seated with the Duke of Edinburgh on thrones under a canopy for the outdoor ceremony on Parliament Hill, Her Majesty proclaimed the revised Canadian Constitution on April 17, 1982. It was a raw Ottawa spring day and a chill wind lashed participants with short bursts of rain. Had the Queen not been there few would have turned up. Once patriation had been settled on, Elizabeth had facilitated the process. Trudeau in his *Memoirs* recalled the Queen's conduct at this time with grudging gratitude: "I was always impressed not only by the grace she displayed in public, but by the wisdom she showed in private conversation." By the final settlement, the constitutional position of Her Majesty as set out by the Fathers of Confederation was unchanged and future alterations to the royal office required unanimous consent of the Senate, the House of Commons, and all ten provincial legislative assemblies.

Elizabeth and Philip were actively involved in the rapidly changing Canada of the 1980s. The constitutional entrenchment of the Monarchy in 1982 was followed by the advent of the Mulroney Government two years later. It proved more sympathetic to the Sovereign. The number of tours initiated by Ottawa, as opposed to provincial invitations approved by the federal government, increased. Many Canadians noted with approval the Queen's comment, "I'm going home to Canada tomorrow," to reporters at the conclusion of her American West Coast visit in 1983. She and Philip received a terrific welcome when they reached British Columbia. As Queen of Canada Elizabeth, together with the Duke, received the French President at the Canadian War Cemetery at Beny-sur-Mer in France the following year for the fortieth anniversary of D-Day, and in the autumn both celebrated the bicentenary of the Loyalists in New Brunswick and Ontario. A brilliantly conceived walkabout in Toronto's Little Italy, before twenty thousand people, showed how the Sovereign could be relevant for immigrant communities in Canada.

Throughout the 1980s the Queen and the Duke continued their policy of sharing their family, the marriages of the younger members having captured the attention of young Canadians. Elizabeth even allowed her mother, the much loved Queen Elizabeth the Queen Mother, to do short tours until finally she reached the age of eighty-nine and her daughter, fearing for her welfare, said no more. A Commonwealth Heads of Government meeting took place in Victoria in 1987 for which Elizabeth and Philip were present, and the royal couple made short tours in British Columbia and Saskatchewan. As part of the Mulroney Cabinet's attempt to reintegrate Quebec into Confederation, the Duke accompanied the Queen on her first official visit to Quebec since 1964. Her purpose was to help the Quebec Premier, Robert Bourassa, demonstrate the reality of the Meech Lake Accord he had reached with Ottawa to Quebecers and the rest of Canada. The visit was a great success. As is her policy, the Queen when asked to support her Government did so, without commenting on specific provisions of the Accord, and subsequent criticism of her action by its opponents was not justified.

Unfortunately the Accord failed just a week before the Queen's next tour, a solo sojourn in Alberta in 1990. At the conclusion of her four days in the West she flew to Ottawa for the Canada Day celebration on Parliament Hill, the first time in many years the Sovereign had been present. Far from avoiding reference to the country's crisis, she confronted it head on. "I am not just a fair weather friend, and I am glad to be here at this sensitive time," she said. She hoped her presence might recall the "many years of shared experience" the country had had "and raise new hopes for the future." Her emotion spoke to the feelings of her compatriots.

The Mulroney years ended in 1993, but not before Elizabeth became the first Sovereign of Canada to give permission under Section 26 of the Constitution Act of 1867 for a government to create additional Senators, which she had to do to enable it to pass the Goods and Services Tax. She also reconstituted the Victoria Cross as part of the new Canadian military decorations, ensuring it remained the country's highest honour for valour under fire. At the 1992 Canada Day, which was the 125th anniversary of Confederation, she was again present in Ottawa, this time also without the Duke, and unveiled the equestrian statue of herself that

Before 18,000 cheering fans the Queen drops the puck in Vancouver during her Golden Jubilee tour.

had been erected on Parliament Hill. Concerns for the country's unity remained paramount and Her Majesty called on all Canadians to cherish their heritage "and protect it with all your strength."

The 1990s was a period of personal anguish and trial for Elizabeth and Philip, with the marriages of three of their children ending in divorce, the Princess of Wales's unexpected death in a car crash, and the decommissioning of the venerable *Britannia.* A welcome contrast was the success of the royal couple's two Canadian tours in 1994 and 1997. Participation by the Queen in an interfaith service at Sydney in Cape Breton, during which there were readings in Hebrew and from the Koran, as well as a New Testament lesson read by the Duke of Edinburgh, showed they were keeping abreast of Canada's changing fabric. During three days in Yellowknife the Queen dedicated the new Legislative Assembly chamber and looked forward to the creation of Nunavut, visiting Rankin Inlet (where the entire population turned out to greet her and the Duke) and Iqaluit on Baffin Island, both of which were to be part of it. The year 1997 marked the five hundredth anniversary of the Crown in Canada, and Elizabeth and Philip were at Bonavista for the arrival of the *Matthew,* the replica of Cabot's original ship of 1497 that was sent on its voyage of discovery by their ancestor King Henry VII.

No one knows better than Elizabeth and Philip that monarchy is not just about tours and happy occasions. It encompasses weightier issues as well: constitutional stability, national identity, social problems, leadership. With the Chrétien Government in office, the Queen found the Canadian political and bureaucratic establishment trotting out the old ideas of Bill C-60 again. Though two separatist governments and two referenda on independence, the second only narrowly defeated, proved that flag, anthem, and nationalist myth had not solved Canada's unity problem, foes of the Crown, their mentality frozen in the 1960s and 1970s, were still trying to replace the Queen with that formula. To be "more Canadian" they wanted Canada distorted from what it was into a copy of other states. The Queen, who values service, family, community, and the greater good, was not politically correct in their view. Nationalism had embraced socio-political liberalism and become an ideology that was about getting not giving, self-serving not self-sacrificing. Projects such as removing or diminishing the Queen in the citizenship oath soon received the official nod.

It is not only "our country" that the Queen can say she has got to know "rather well." She has come to understand her Canadians just as closely. At Regina in 2005 Elizabeth listened to her tenth and short-lived Prime Minister, Paul Martin, welcome her by saying, "we give to you, as always, our loyalty, our deep affection." So shrewd an observer as Elizabeth II could not fail to notice that the politician publicly offering her his loyalty barely five months before had removed her name from the letters of credence and recall of Canadian ambassadors. If the Queen after dealing with so many Canadian politicians has learned to take such behaviour in context, she must have found it more difficult to accept and cope with it in yet another place.

In the most recent phase of the reign, it has become increasingly clear that the place where loyalty to the Queen of Canada ought to be paramount, namely Rideau Hall, the residence of her official representative, has become a major force in undermining the Sovereign's position. Appointed by the Queen, a Governor General is by definition a deputy, not a rival, and swears or solemnly affirms to "well and truly serve Her Majesty Queen Elizabeth

"I treasure my place in the life of Canada and my bond with Canadians everywhere," the Queen told a Vancouver audience in her Golden Jubilee year.

II" while in office. On retiring as Governor General in 1979, Jules Léger sent a farewell message to the provincial lieutenant-governors urging them to continue "working for the enhancement of Canada, a portion of which has been entrusted to each of you on behalf of Her Gracious Majesty the Queen of Canada, whose faithful servants we all are."

The Queen would search in vain for such fidelity today. Like Lady Macduff does in answering her young son's question "What is a traitor?" in *Macbeth*, she could say "Why, one that swears and lies." She has certainly found little commitment to her in her most recent viceregal representatives. Adrienne Clarkson when Governor General actually suggested to the Palace that she take precedence over the Queen at the Juno Beach commemoration in 2004. It was like the Deputy Prime Minister wanting to precede the Prime Minister. When the Queen invited Michaëlle Jean to her eightieth birthday party two years later, Her Excellency refused to go but found time to rush off to Haiti for the inauguration of its latest president.

It is virtually impossible for the Queen to combat and refute fabrications about the Monarchy circulated by ministers of her government or by viceregal staff. The latter for example glibly state that the Sovereign handed over all the powers of the Crown to the Governor General by the Letters Patent of 1947. The Letters do not say so; they simply allow the Queen's representative to exercise those powers. But the Queen, Government House would have Canadians think, is prohibited from acting abroad for Canada or carrying out any constitutional functions within the country. If so, why did the Government of Louis St. Laurent have the Queen open Parliament in 1957 and the Trudeau Government arrange for her to do it again in 1977?

The Queen is a professional, conditioned by birth, thoroughly trained, with a solid record of achievement. Foes of the Crown want to replace her with an ex-politician, prominent media personage, or popular figure plucked from some other sphere. To expect that such people, able to support the Queen as her assistants, could actually replace Her Majesty with the same success is naive and belied by the trial runs, for recent viceregal representatives have seen themselves as substitutes and have failed. The Queen for example would never have been so self-indulgent as to plead exhaustion, as Michaëlle Jean did, to avoid swearing in new government ministers, one of the Monarch's most important functions. Nor would Elizabeth have been so constitutionally ignorant as to talk about "dissolving the Government" instead of correctly saying "dissolving Parliament" as Jean did before the 2006 election. The Queen has navigated through delicate and sensitive situations without once compromising the non-partisan record of her office, but Jean at her installation publicly thanked the partisan Prime Minister instead of the Queen for appointing her. The Prime Minister *nominates* and the Sovereign *appoints* the person chosen as Governor General, confirming the impartiality of the office despite the political advice.

Nor is the case of Jean an isolated one. Other recent viceregal representatives have shown similar misunderstandings of their role. Adrienne Clarkson brought the Crown into controversy in 2004 by her unexplained expenditures; Jean Sauvé was so paranoid about her security that she barred the

A marriage partnership of sixty successful years that continues to work for Canada.

public from the Rideau Hall grounds and spent most of her time in Montreal; and Roméo LeBlanc created a silly and unnecessary uproar over the Royal Crest of Canada by deciding to depict the lion without its tongue because he foolishly thought it was offensive. When a Governor General no longer thinks he is representing the Queen, he has to create a whole new role for himself and gets into trouble doing so. Is it any wonder Stephen Harper wanted the Queen, who understands her role perfectly and can be depended upon to carry it out faultlessly, at the important ceremony on Vimy Ridge?

The Queen is still proud and happy to be Queen of Canada, though one might understand if she felt

The state is the permanent Canada. However much the people of the country change ethnically, religiously, or linguistically, the Queen remains constant as its embodiment. Royal Canadian Mint postcard marking a new effigy of the Sovereign for Canadian coinage, 2003 (above). The Queen at a Government of Canada dinner in Edmonton, 2005 (left).

otherwise, having received so much disloyalty, abuse, ingratitude, and offhand disrespect from her political servants. One of the saddest passages in her reign in Canada is how, when her right to approve appointments to the Order of Canada was abruptly terminated, she appealed to be allowed at least to continue to know the names of the people appointed. She was interested in her Canadians and wanted to be kept informed. She puts the country ahead of her own interests. When the Harper Government in 2006 proposed restoring her name to the diplomatic letters of credence and recall, the Queen expressed concern that it might become a political football. It is because Elizabeth has given so much to the country and because she vowed to do so all her life that she has not changed her feelings about it. "I treasure my place in the life of Canada and my bond with Canadians everywhere," she said in Vancouver during her Golden Jubilee celebration in 2002. For her part she will never go back on that promise or retract that love. She feels she belongs to Canada and she also "feels Canadian," as a biographer of mid-reign put it. Her fidelity is not merely reluctance to break an old family tie, either, though she knows full well how her family helped create and gave an identity to Canada, which but for the Crown would be part of the United States.

Philip's feelings are more difficult to pin down. He is undemonstrative by nature and though in his completely unstuffy way given to calling a spade a spade and raising people's ire because of it, he has as the Consort of the Queen of Canada through many a touchy situation been utterly discreet and never by any careless word or breach of confidence caused any embarrassment or difficulty for the Queen, and without that caution, the Queen's job would have been more difficult. He never would abandon the country to which his wife is so deeply committed. He must have been furious to witness the disloyalty shown his wife and Queen — for instance, during the Golden Jubilee tour in 2002, John Manley, a Chrétien Cabinet member, attacked the Monarchy, and a couple of days later he was the Minister in Attendance on Her Majesty, when he should have been fired for breaching his oath and insulting his Sovereign. The Prince's only sign of ire was a curt "Stand over there!" to Manley at the royal arrival in Ottawa.

Elizabeth has had the added vexation of seeing Philip her beloved consort treated with a double standard. Reflecting gender equality, Canadian protocol provides that male as well as female spouses of the Governor General are automatically appointed to the Order of Canada, and yet the spouse of the Queen who is Sovereign of the Order does not get the same treatment. According to journalists His Royal Highness was offered honorary membership, the category of the Order reserved for foreigners, but indignantly refused because he is no alien. Indeed as the member of the Royal Family who holds the all-time record for Canadian tours, stays, and stopovers — nearly eighty in all — he might well think so. As for his feelings, he once commented in a speech on his state of mind on crossing from the United States to Canada, "I somehow belong on this side."

The marriage of Elizabeth and Philip has been a very modern one. Since 1947 they both have been working professionals, long before such a pattern became normal for most married people, and have felt all the attendant stresses, problems, and hardships. Yet within that relationship they have complemented and supported each other effectively and loyally. Perhaps working at different aspects of the same job has helped. The partnership has been the key to their success in Canada. Whatever the political and bureaucratic establishment may think, it is a remarkable achievement for the Queen to have reigned in the contentious "Kingdom of the North" for more than fifty-five years without ever losing the people's respect, affection, and loyalty. Cheerful, unflinching service has compelled the esteem of a public more easily beguiled by superstar glamour. The vocation Her Majesty and her husband share is an important one. Many Canadians again realized what the Queen has to offer in 2005 when she arrived in Regina for the centenaries of the provinces of Saskatchewan and Alberta. The country was mired in the federal sponsorship scandal but her appearance at once lifted official life to a higher plane beyond partisanship and corruption, which is where Canada deserves to have it.

9
Modern Age, Modern Marriage

"[Prince Philip] has been my strength and stay all these years"
— *Queen Elizabeth II in her golden wedding anniversary speech*

"Tolerance," stated the Duke of Edinburgh at his golden wedding anniversary celebration, "is the one essential ingredient of any happy marriage." The Queen, he added, has that quality in abundance. Mutual compliments aside, for a royal marriage to be successful and happy there is no doubt that accommodation is a necessity. Over the long period of sixty years the marriage of Elizabeth and Philip, about which a great deal has been written, has indeed been distinguished by a succession of skilful adjustments.

The royal couple are adept at making adjustments because they have done so from the very beginning. Adversity, however unappealing it is in prospect, is the best school for life — at least for those capable of learning from it, and Elizabeth and Philip both were, in the private as well as the public sphere. The world war that disrupted their lives for six long years was not their only ordeal. Princess Elizabeth's childhood was abruptly changed at age ten by King Edward VIII's abdication and her life as a young married woman by her father's premature death fifteen years later, while Prince Philip's character was forged in revolution, separated parents, and a peripatetic boyhood. It might be thought that Elizabeth as Heiress Presumptive to the Throne led a sheltered life and was immune to it all, but that was not the case; she had to fight her own battle for her love and for her personal freedom within the context of her vocation. As Philip Lacey, a biographer of the Queen, puts it, "Both [Elizabeth and Philip], in a sense, were old beyond their years," and that was because of what life to that point had brought them.

The royal couple were two such different characters that there was no given mutual compatibility to guarantee marital success. Queen Elizabeth II is rather a shy, self-contained person, never one to

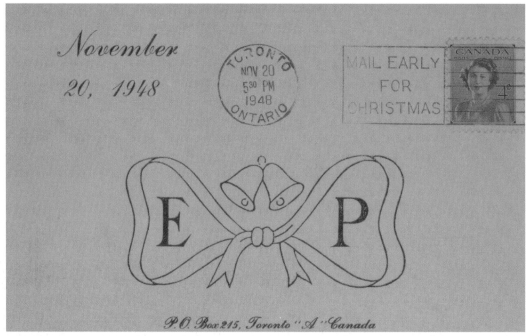

A Canadian postcard marking the first wedding anniversary of Princess Elizabeth and the Duke of Edinburgh.

wear her heart on her sleeve, and conservative by nature. She is clever though not an intellectual. Generally described as lacking in imagination (no liability to a constitutional monarch), she is nevertheless a sharp observer. A serious and well-disciplined person, she is capable of hard work, able to read masses of state papers and understand and master them in detail. In short the Queen is a thoroughly professional woman, always on top of her job, in which she takes delight and pride and does extremely well. She has the queenly if not the common touch. When, as a girl, she grasped her vocation, she found it meaningful and has never changed her mind about it. The Queen is also blessed in possessing a sense of humour and fun that has been a great help to her.

Her husband, Prince Philip, Duke of Edinburgh, is quite a different type. By nature he is possessed of keen intelligence and energy. Having been forged in a hard school his is a tough character and that, suggests Ben Pimlott, another recent biographer of Her Majesty, is why the Queen fell in love with him. Ambition to achieve is one of his dominant characteristics, and throughout his life he has identified his goals and gone all out to achieve them, cutting through the obstacles that stood in his way. Like many people who see the world in clear terms and know their destination, the Prince is impulsive and impatient of delays, red tape, and stupidity. Possessing a short temper, quick wit, and sharp tongue, he appears and often is testy, abrasive, and querulous.

Tender concern for the young Princess Elizabeth is shown on the face of her husband as they leave the reviewing stand at Wolfe's Cove, Quebec City, on October 9, 1951. In the background is the Royal 22e Régiment guard of honour.

Philip does not have a romantic or a sentimental view of life. Quite the reverse; he is attracted by the practical side of existence as his early and continuing interest in science and technology showed. His habit of questioning, probing, and arguing in order to understand and provoke answers, together with a certain decisive strain, suited him for the naval career that he successfully adopted, and his natural inclinations were in turn enhanced and developed by it. Contemporary prejudice against monarchy should not obscure the influence heredity has had in forming a character that has the ability and inclination to lead and to command. Philip in short remains a blunt, unstuffy, no-nonsense naval officer.

Whatever its shortcomings, his way of dealing with life has led to his becoming a highly successful speaker, author, and pioneer advocate of many important causes. Lady Longford was on the right track when she wrote in her *Elizabeth R* that

> Philip's "arrogance" is no more than the impatience of a doer with obfuscators — the occasional rough manners of one who has never learnt to suffer fools gladly, or a touch of the royal naval chaff that was so apparent in Edward VII and George V. Real arrogance implies a layer of self-satisfaction, of conceit. Prince Philip is not guilty, partly because he is as little introspective or concerned with himself as he is intensely focused on an external achievement.

In two such different characters as Elizabeth's and Philip's there was plenty of potentially combustible material, but between them there was also love, attraction, and a serious attitude towards the vows they exchanged on their wedding day and the future commitments they were to make to each other. The first challenges to their marriage came with the need to set up their households and staff. Well-intentioned and eager to put his experience, wisdom, and skill at the service of the Heiress Presumptive and her husband, the Duke's revered uncle Earl Mountbatten of Burma sought in Philip's words to become "the General Manager of this little show," and his nephew had to explain to him that the Princess might not "take to the idea quite as docilely as I do." This was the beginning of Prince Philip's long record of shielding his wife.

In the first four and a half years of Elizabeth and Philip's marriage, it was the Princess who had to adjust to the claims of her husband's profession as a naval officer. She did it quite well. When the Duke worked at the Admiralty in London, Elizabeth often cooked the meals in their flat at Kensington Palace on the servants' day off and he helped with the washing up. In 1949 Philip was appointed to the Mediterranean Fleet at Malta and in July 1950 given his first command, the frigate HMS *Magpie*. Combining royal and wifely duties, Princess Elizabeth moved back and forth between Clarence House in London and Malta. The couple's period in Malta was a new experience for the future Queen and was the one time in which she was enabled to live a normal life as a naval officer's wife. "She spent only ten per cent of her time being a Princess," said the Duke's friend and equerry, the Australian Commander Michael Parker. From their residence, the Villa Guardamangia, she went shopping, attended hotel dances, associated with other naval wives, and got away on yacht trips, picnics, and swimming expeditions.

This was also the time when the royal couple had Clarence House as their official abode. Clarence House was the first real home the Duke had had in his twenty-eight years so it is no wonder that the period there from 1949 to 1952 was one of the happiest in all the places they have lived in their married life. Pimlott has described the Clarence House household as "a happy, close-knit group of helpers, over which the influence of the busy and contented Princess shone."

At her wedding Princess Elizabeth had promised

Their days in Malta were the only period of their married life when Elizabeth and Philip were able to live normally without media intrusion.

to "obey" her husband. For her the vow was deliberate and no empty one. Knowing the demands and prominence her public role gave her, Elizabeth was determined in order to keep a balance in their marital relationship that Philip should be treated as a traditional male head of the family, as husband and father. Through thick and thin, she has never deviated from this determination and it was a wise policy because Philip soon had to make the greatest sacrifice of all to their marriage: abandonment in

1951 of his naval career. "I make no secret of the fact that I enjoyed my time in the Royal Navy," he told his biographer Basil Boothroyd twenty years later. The King's illness, however, made it clear that Princess Elizabeth and her husband would have to take on extra duties and doing so would be incompatible with continuing his naval life. It is generally agreed that Philip, had he continued in the navy, would ultimately have achieved the rank of First Sea Lord, so the sacrifice he made was a considerable one and keenly felt. Not surprisingly his valet, John Dean, found "the Duke was inclined to be moody and impatient when we first came home from Malta." But the renunciation was in keeping with what Philip told Michael Parker at the time of his engagement: "This is my destiny, to support my wife in what lies ahead for her." The shock was that it came so much earlier than anticipated.

Perhaps the most serious challenge to the relationship of Elizabeth and Philip as a married couple was the Queen's accession to the Throne in February 1952. Having a Queen Regnant was an exception to the historic pattern of monarchy in which kings predominate, and bringing with it a male consort whose role was undefined created further uncertainty. Not only did Elizabeth's being Queen increase the tempo of the royal couple's life and cut short a normal existence for them, but it also tipped the balance hazardously within the marriage. Henceforth they were to be involved in a routine of public duties and constant scrutiny by the media that death alone could end. Because she was Queen, everyone now went to Elizabeth, whereas up to 1952 many went as Her Majesty wished to the Duke as head of the family.

Moving into Buckingham Palace brought Philip the innovator into an environment hostile to change, a hostility great even though often veiled or unarticulated. This became especially clear when the Duke let it be known that the staid Palace needed to be made more efficient and brought closer to the needs of contemporary life. In keeping with what he saw as his mission as the Queen's husband, Philip had to persuade the royal household to bring to him some of the problems and matters from which a woman would normally be excused.

In the new situation the Queen's chief adviser, her private secretary, could sometimes be the rival of her husband. Two public slights to her husband — the decision that the royal house would continue to be called the House of Windsor and not change its name to that of Philip's family and the placing of a chair of estate for him outside the canopy over the Sovereign's Throne when the Queen opened her first Parliament — could not be prevented by the inexperienced young Monarch. "I am the only man in the country not allowed to give his name to his children," the Duke purportedly remarked. But remembering his determination not to get involved in controversy over constitutional and political matters he contented himself with writing a memorandum on the subject. The Queen realized her husband had been snubbed but was not able to make it up to him for some time. Was it any wonder that Philip, thick-skinned as he was, absented himself from meetings of the Privy Council and other more formal and traditional occasions?

A growing (and still unsolved) problem of the reign, one that was to have its impact on Elizabeth and Philip's entire sixty years of married life, was media militancy and intrusiveness. Though it would grow to the point of ruthlessly exploiting the unhappiness of a member of their family, their daughter-in-law Diana, Princess of Wales, and threatening family solidarity, its popping flash bulbs and miles of film were there at the time of their wedding too. "You pick a wife, and half the world, as of right, joins in," complained Philip, remembering those early days. It was being trailed by journalists whose reports brought crowds where otherwise there would have been none that disturbed Elizabeth at the time of her engagement, turning the public functions that had brought her pleasure into trials. Wisely, the Queen ignored media-encouraged discussions about whether it was possible to be the Queen and a mother at the same time.

Philip continued developing his support plan, his role of interpreting the outside world to the Queen, assisting her with her speeches and broadcasts, blazing new trails as he gradually focused his attention on youth development and the environment. His interests and activities took him to all parts of the far-flung Commonwealth. The longest trip he made, 40,000 miles in 140 days mainly on board the *Britannia*, lasted from mid-October 1956 to mid-February of the following year. His itinerary included Malaya, New Zealand, Ceylon, Gambia, Antarctica, and the Galapagos, in addition to Australia, where the Duke opened the Olympic Games in Melbourne, the first ever held south of the equator.

The Queen's husband clearly had established his presence in the United Kingdom, for his absence while he was on this voyage was noticed and became a subject of controversy. The Suez crisis was being played out at the start of the tour. Because one purpose of the trip was to make royal visits to many places in the Commonwealth that had never had one, it went ahead. In her 1956 Christmas broadcast the Queen said, "If my husband cannot be at home on Christmas Day, I could not wish for a better reason than that he should be travelling in other parts of the Commonwealth." But the British media, well on its course of hypocritical self-righteousness, after generally ignoring the tour finally decided to depict it as a pleasure jaunt for Philip and his entourage. In the ensuing uproar there was something of the little England mentality that looks on the Crown as a British preserve generously lent from time to time to other Commonwealth countries instead of being equally their property and heritage. By this time too the bloom was wearing off the unusual popularity that Elizabeth and Philip had enjoyed since their engagement.

When *Britannia* reached Gibraltar on its home journey in February 1957, the Duke remained on board instead of flying on to London. His reason was that the Queen was about to make a state visit to nearby Portugal and he had arranged to join her there. The *Sunday Pictorial*, a British newspaper, launched an attack on the Duke for being a bad father because he did not rush home to his wife and children. An American paper, *The Baltimore Sun*, printed a completely fabricated story about an alleged romantic involvement of Philip's with the headline "Queen, Duke in Rift Over Party Girl." According to the press rumour mill the Queen was upset and the Commonwealth tour had been organized to provide for the royal couple's separation. The media of course was unaware

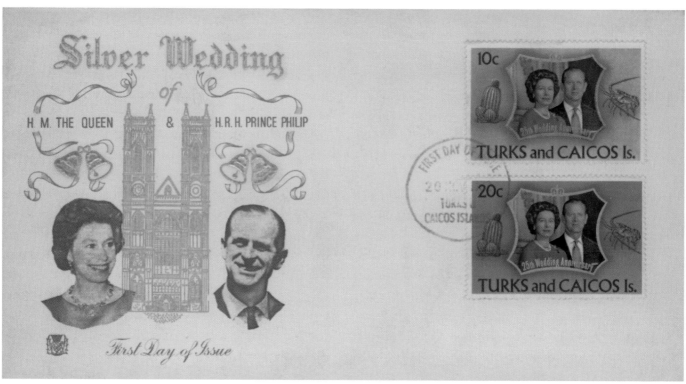

Turks and Caicos Islands first day cover issued for the Queen and the Duke's silver wedding anniversary in 1972.

that during the voyage Philip had sent his wife white roses on their ninth wedding anniversary and regularly spoke to the Queen, Prince Charles, and Princess Anne by telephone. Another chance ingredient in this tempest in a teapot was the fact that Commander Parker, the Duke's loyal and effective equerry of ten years, was being sued for divorce by his wife and felt he had to resign.

Faced with direct attack on the stability of her marriage, Elizabeth II ordered a denial to be issued. "It is quite untrue that there is any rift between the Queen and the Duke of Edinburgh," said the statement from the Palace. Parker recalled that Philip was "very, very angry. And deeply hurt."

Though the statement calmed the storm, issuing a denial put the question of the royal marriage into the public domain. Elizabeth and Philip were reunited according to plan at Lisbon Airport, and later in a London speech the Duke justified his tour, stating that there were "some things for which it is worthwhile making some personal sacrifices" and he believed the "Commonwealth is one of these things." Making her own feelings about her husband clear, the Queen marked their tenth wedding anniversary that year by creating Philip a Prince of the United Kingdom to recognize the already outstanding contribution he had made to the life and welfare of the Commonwealth.

The birth of Prince Andrew in 1960 and Prince Edward in 1964 was sufficient proof of the continuing good relations between the royal couple to ward off media fantasies. Twenty-five years after the 1957 affair, on July 9, 1982, the bizarre incident of the intrusion of Michael Fagan, a thirty-five-year-old, unemployed, schizophrenic man with family troubles, into the Palace occurred. Media stories paid deserved tribute to the calm courage and presence of mind displayed by the Queen when confronted with this unfortunate individual whose object was to commit suicide in front of Her Majesty. Soon, however, the question of why Prince Philip was not there at the time overshadowed everything else. The implication was that the Queen and the Duke no longer had normal conjugal relations. Unpleasant as the Fagan incident was for the Queen, and shameful for those entrusted with Palace security, it gave the public an unexpected glimpse into the state of the royal marriage. The Palace in response to speculation made it quite clear that when the Queen and the Duke sleep under the same roof they normally do share the same bed. On this particular occasion, the Duke had spent the night in his own quarters because he was leaving for an early engagement and did not wish to disturb his wife's sleep. The public further learned that ever since Elizabeth and Philip had taken up residence at Clarence House a year and a half after their wedding they'd had separate but adjoining rooms. Though it was a subject neither Queen nor Duke would ever have discussed, in this way they confirmed the healthy state of their marriage.

It is ironic and pitiful that such a successful marriage as the Queen and the Duke's, which might serve as an example for the age, has been the plaything of the media of every sort. The wildest stories have been spun, including infidelities by the Duke and allegations that the Duke is not the father of Andrew and Edward. Gyles Brandreth, the sanest and most balanced recent biographer of the royal couple, deals painstakingly with the question in his *Philip and Elizabeth: Portrait of a Royal Marriage.* His conclusion is that the Duke has been completely faithful to the Queen, and he quotes Countess Mountbatten as saying, "I'm sure of it, completely and utterly sure." The Duke is not one to talk about his feelings or his intimate life, nor is the Queen, who anyway could not. He has, however, said privately that the thing would be impossible, surrounded as he constantly is with security people. "How could I be unfaithful to the Queen?" he asked, answering his own question as a man of honour would, "There is no way she could possibly retaliate." Brandreth firmly concludes, "The Duke of Edinburgh's conscience is clear." All who have said otherwise, be they media, courtiers, writers, or associates, have failed to produce a shred of evidence to prove it.

As they approach their sixtieth wedding anniversary, the Queen and the Duke of Edinburgh are clearly comfortable and relaxed in their marriage. Whereas the Duke does not talk about their relationship, the Queen wants all the world to know that her heart has belonged to her husband since she was thirteen. Both remain undemonstrative in public, though this self-restraint has been less strict ever since the 1980s when they mischievously caught most of the media off guard and gave each other a kiss at Ottawa Airport following the proclamation of the revised Canadian Constitution as they left the

Relaxed moment for the royal couple in the 1970s.

capital to go their separate ways.

Within the bounds of marriage each has developed and matured while remaining a distinct person. The Queen who earlier suffered her husband's impatient and harsh outbursts in silence has learned to tease him out of such moods when they come upon him, just as she developed what Robert Lacey reports the Duke as calling her "dog mechanism" — taking the corgis for long walks, bringing them home, washing them, and taking them out again — to cope with the frustrations she faces. The Duke's stature and place in history is assured. He has made a success of all the public ventures into which he put so much time and thought. *The Times* has congratulated him for being "a specialist in saying the unsayable" and called him

"a national treasure." "His manner has made him stand out as an individual," another commentator, the publisher Nigel Nicolson, has said, "and he has contributed an image to the Monarchy which is quite different from that of any other royal person, historical or abroad."

His own peppery nature goes hand in hand with a self-deprecating quality and he describes his achievements quite modestly. "I've been lectured to by all the experts in a great many fields, and inevitably something has stuck," he once joked. He can be genuinely modest because he has no craving for praise and does not really care what the world thinks. Being part of a successful marriage has not stifled his individuality but rather has offered him the perspective it needed in which to flourish.

When the Queen left Ottawa after proclaiming the revised Canadian Constitution, the Duke who was off to a different destination gave his wife a goodbye kiss. The kiss caught the media off guard because the royal couple had not until then been accustomed to display emotion in public.

Elizabeth and Philip carry out many ceremonial occasions such as the annual Garter Ceremony at Windsor Castle together.

Besides his love for his wife, he knows in his capacity as Prince and successful naval officer as much about duty as does the Queen. It was unromantic Philip who provided the Coronation with one of its most moving moments when he knelt and pledged fealty to his wife who was also his Queen. "I Philip, Duke of Edinburgh, do become your liegeman of life and limb and of earthly worship; and faith and truth I will bear unto you, to live and die against all manner of folks," he said, rose, kissed Her Majesty, and touched her crown.

Even so the Duke of Edinburgh is still not well understood, something made clear by the grossly inadequate portrayal of him in the acclaimed 2006 film *The Queen*. He has nonetheless remained the head of the family, "the firm's boss in family matters," for the Queen continued her method of making it up to him that she adopted at the beginning of the reign by deferring to him as supreme in the family domain. She gave him the say in the education of their children and put him in charge of the Sandringham and Balmoral estates. This role was clear in the sad breakup of the Prince and Princess of Wales's marriage. It was the Duke who acted on behalf of the royal couple in trying to heal the breach and dealt with Diana by writing her

Philip listens thoughtfully as his wife speaks to more than nine hundred people in Toronto at a Government of Canada gala dinner.

The Duke of Edinburgh hands the Queen a knife to cut a cake at the Canada Day Seniors Celebration in Lansdowne Park, Ottawa, to mark the fiftieth year of their marriage.

A happy Queen and Duke at the service of thanksgiving at Westminster Abbey for their golden wedding anniversary, November 20, 1997.

long and wise letters. He even arranged a session that he and the Queen held with Charles and Diana in an effort to sort out their marital problems and let them know he and the Queen understood such difficulties. When this failed he acted with the Queen to support their son and in the process strove to be fair to Diana. What could show better the degree to which he held the trust of his wife? "You'd better speak to Prince Philip. He's the one she listens to," was the advice of his son Prince Edward to someone who wanted the Queen to do something.

Because the Queen cannot speak about

personal affairs without compromising the dignity she believes a monarch must have, the public sees the royal marriage mainly through the eyes of the Duke who can and does react and comment. Individuals who purposefully pursue happiness seldom find it, whereas those who get on with life and do their duty and work for the welfare of others often find they are happy without having yearned for the state. This is the case with Queen Elizabeth II and Prince Philip, Duke of Edinburgh. In the end steady, faithful service to each other has counted most for the success the royal couple have made of their sixty-year marriage, just as their service to so many peoples around the world has enabled them from the top of the pinnacle to effect good in such a wide spectrum of life.

Bibliography

Allison, Ronald and Sarah Riddell. *The Royal Encyclopedia*, 1991.

Arch, Nigel and Joanna Marschner. *The Royal Wedding Dresses*, 1990.

Boothroyd, Basil. *Prince Philip: An Informal Biography*, 1971.

Bousfield, Arthur and Garry Toffoli. *Fifty Years The Queen: A Tribute To Her Majesty Queen Elizabeth II On Her Golden Jubilee*, 2002.

Bousfield, Arthur and Garry Toffoli. *The Queen Mother and Her Century: An Illustrated Biography Of Queen Elizabeth The Queen Mother On Her 100th Birthday*, 2000.

Bradford, Sarah. *Elizabeth: A Biography of Her Majesty The Queen*, 1996.

Brandreth, Gyles. *Philip & Elizabeth: Portrait Of A Royal Marriage*, 2004.

Campbell, Lady Colin. *The Royal Marriages: Private Lives of the Queen and her Children*, 1993.

Dean, John. *H.R.H. Prince Philip, Duke of Edinburgh: A Portrait by his Valet*, 1956.

Green, David. *Queen Anne*, 1970.

Heald, Tim. *The Duke: A Portrait of Prince Philip*, 1991.

Hoey, Brian. *Snowdon: Public Figure, Private Man*, 2005.

Hume, Martin. *Two English Queens and Philip*, 1903.

Liversidge, Douglas. *Prince Philip: First Gentleman of the Realm*, 1976.

Longford, Elizabeth. *Elizabeth R: A Biography*, 1983.

McCreery, Christopher. *The Order of Canada: Its Origins, History, and Development*, 2005.

Phillips, Melanie. *Londonistan*, 2006.

Roll, Winifred. *Mary I: The History Of An Unhappy Tudor Queen*, 1980.

Seward, Ingrid. *The Queen & Di*, 2000.

Stone, J.M. *The History of Mary I Queen Of England*, 1901.

Turner, Graham. *Elizabeth: The Woman and the Queen*, 2002.

Vickers, Hugo. *Alice: Princess Andrew of Greece*, 2000.

Worwick, Christopher. *Two Centuries of Royal Weddings*, 1980.

Index

Pages numbers in *italics* = mention in caption

Aberfan, Wales, 93, *94*
Adelaide, Queen (Princess of Saxe-Meiningen), 58
Aden, 126
Admiralty, 79, 116, 132, 133
Afghanistan, 139, 140
Africa, 127
Air travel, 131
Albert the Prince Consort, 54, *59*, 60, 71, 79–83, *80, 81, 82*, 85, *86*, 87, 97, 129, 131
Albert Victor, Prince, Duke of Clarence, 30, 46, *46*, 47
Alberta, 100, 161
Alexander III, 75
Alexandra, Queen, 27, 31, 60
Alexandra, Princess, 17, 54, *65*, 67
Alexandra, Empress (Alix of Hesse), *50*
Alice, Princess Andrew of Greece, 14, 26, 28, *28*, 29, 39, 40, 44, 107, 108, *110*
Alice, Duchess of Gloucester, 45, *45*
Al-Qaeda, 94
Andrew, Prince, of Greece, 28, *28*, 29, 30, 35, 39, 44, 107
Andrew, Prince, Duke of York, *68*, 69, 103, 104, 111, 112, *113*, 114, 120, 147, 152, 171
Anne, Queen, 71, 78–79, *79*, 84
Anne of Denmark, Queen, 51, *53*
Anne, Princess Royal (Princess William of Orange), 51
Anne, Princess Royal, 63, *66*, *93*, 103, 110, *110*, 111, *111*, 112, *113*, 114, 117, 132, *151*, 170
Annus horribilis, 112
Asia, 127
Antigua and Barbuda, 123
Arch, Nigel, 67
Arthur, King, 72
Arthur, Prince, 47
Attlee, Clement, 11
Atlantic, 38, 132, 134
ATS (Auxiliary Territorial Service), 24, 38
Australia, 32, 35, 38, 96, 101, 104, 123, 124, 126, 131, 133
Australian State, Queen as embodiment of, 125
Australian State Coach, *124*
Austria, 74
Bagehot, Walter, 107, 138
Bahamas, *101*, 123, 126
Baldwin, Stanley, 34
Balmoral Castle, 24, 26, 33, 39, 115
Baltic, 134
Barbados, 123
Battenberg, Prince Henry of, 61
Battenberg, Prince Louis of SEE Milford Haven
Battenbergs become Mountbattens, 29
BBC, 23, 113
Beach Boys, 104
Beaton, Sir Cecil, 16

Beatrice, Princess (Princess Henry of Battenberg), 43, 61
Beatrice, Princess, of York, 104, 118, *119*
Belgium, Prince Regent of, 13
Belize, 123
Bennett, R.B., 33
Bennett, Tony, 104
Bermuda, 126
Bernhardt, Prince, 14
Bill C-60, 154
Bill of Divorce, 56
Birkhall, 26, 32
Blackheath, 56
Blair, Tony, 102
Blitz, 37
Bonaparte, Marie, Princess George of Greece, 30
Bois de Boulongne, 30
Bothwell, James Hepburn, Earl of, 71, *76*, 77
Botticelli, Sandro, 16
Brabant, 74
Brabourne, Lord, 116
Brandreth, Gyles, 30, 97, 110
Britannia, HMY, 126, 131, 132, 147, 157, 169
British Airways, 89
British Columbia, *19*, 100, 121, 152, 155
British Empire, 33, 37, 105
British Parliament, 129
Broadlands, 26, 67
Brunswick, 54
Brunswick, House of (House of Hanover), 85
Bruton Street, Number 17, 31, *31*
Bryan, James, 113
Buckingham Palace, 17, 24, 26, 31, 37, 39, 43, 45, 60, 62, 69, 94, *95*, 98, 102, *103*, 104, 105, 108, 110, *111*, 119, *124*
Burgundy, 74
Burma, 19
Bush, George H., 127
Bush, George W., 105, 126, 127
Calais, 75
Cambridge University, 81
Cambridge, Duke of, 45, 57
Cambridge, Lady May, *69*
Camelot, 71
Camilla Parker Bowles, Duchess of Cornwall, 115
Canada, 19, 33, 34, 35, 37, 63, 82, *87*, *97*, 100, 104, 108, 114, 118, 123, 124, 125, 126, 130, 132, 133, 134, 140, 142, 143
Canadian Citizenship Act, 85
Canadian Constitution, 154, 155, 156, 158, 171, *173*
Canadian Guards, 145
Canadian North, 100, *145*, 151, 152
Canadian Parliament, 129, 135, 145, *146*, *149*, 152
Canadian State, Queen as embodiment of, 125
Canadian State Landau, *124*
Canterbury, Archbishop of, 23, 24, 49, 115

Canterbury Cathedral, 52
Carlton House, 56
Carney, Kathleen, 90
Caroline, Queen (Caroline of Brunswick), 51, 54, 55, *55*, 56, 59
Carter, Jimmy, 127
Catherine of Bragazna, Queen, 52
Cecile, Princess (Grand Duchess George of Hesse), 108
Ceylon (Sri Lanka), 126
Chapel Royal, St. James's Palace, 47, 56, 60
Chapel Royal, Whitehall Palace, 48
Charles I, 52, *53*
Charles II, 48, 49, 52
Charles V, 73, 74
Charles, Prince of Wales, 11, 59, *67*, 85, 103, 104, 105, 107, 110, *110*, 111, 112, *112*, 114, 115, 116, *116*, 119, *119*, *121*, 131, 132, 147, 152, 170, 175, 176
Charlotte, Queen, 49, *50*, 51, *59*, 60
Cheam School, Surrey, 30, 119
Chiang Kai Shek, President, 19
China, 128
Chrétien, Jean, 157, 161
Christian IX, 27
Christendom, 51
Christmas broadcast, 129
Christmas tree, 82
Churchill, Admiral George, 79
Churchill, John, Duke of Marlborough, 79
Churchill, Sir Winston, 11, 79
Church of England, 23, 114, 115
Clarence House, 18; white Canadian maple for Philip's study at, *18*, 19; *166*, 171
Clarkson, Adrienne, 158, 159
Clinton, William, 127
Cocos Islands, 126
Collegiate School Wanganui, 131
Colville, Jock, 17
Commonwealth, 33, 34, 49, 50, 62, 71, 94, 100, 102, 104–105, 107, *113*, 123, 126, 127, 129, 131, 132, 133, 134, 142, 148, 152, 169, 170
Connaught, Prince Arthur, 1st Duke of, 43
Connaught, Princess Patricia of (Lady Patricia Ramsay), 63
Consorts, male, 71, 87–88
Constantine I, 28, 35
Corfu, 27, 29, *29*
Coronation of 1702, 79; of 1821, 56; of 1937, 35; of 1953, 63, 85, *86*, *108*, 110, 126, 129, 131, 134, 137, 138, 143, 144, 145, 175
Counsellor of State, 85
Coward, Sir Noel, 23
Crawford, Marion "Crawfie", 16, 24, 32, 36, 38, *40*
Creevey, Thomas, 57
Cumberland, Duke of SEE Denmark, Prince George of

Cumberland, Duke of, 54
Cumberland, Ernest, Duke of (King of Hanover), 57
Daimler, Queen Mary's, 21
Darnley, Henry Stuart, Lord, 71, 75, *76*, 77, 85
Dauphin of France, 47
Demonologi, 52
Declaration of Independence (American), 126, *127*
Delicate Investigation, 56
Denmark, 41, 83
Denmark, Prince George of, 71, 78–79, *79*
Denmark, King of, 13
Denmark, Queen of, 13
De St. Laurent, Julie, 57
Diana, Princess of Wales, 11, 59, 63, *67*, *100*, 112, *112*, 113, 115, 116, *116*, *157*, *169*, *175*, *176*
Diana: Her True Story, 113
Diefenbaker, John, 85, 144
Dimbleby, Jonathan, 112
District of Columbia, 105
Downing Street, Number 10, 102
Drake, Sir Francis, 72
Duke of Edinburgh's Award Scheme, 98, 99, 100, *100*, 102, *114*
Dunblane, Scotland, 92, *93*
Dunlop, Rt Revd Alistair, 89, 102
Eardly-Howard-Crockett Prize, 35
E-boat Alley, 38
Edinburgh, Prince Alfred, Duke of Coburg, Duke of, 27, 48, 61
Edinburgh, Marie, Duchess of (Grand Duchess Marie), 48, 61
Edinburgh, Princess Marie of, 47
Edward I, *53*, 54, 75, 76
Edward II, 75
Edward III, 56
Edward VI, 73, 76
Edward VII, 13, 30, 47, 60, *61*, 85
Edward the Black Prince, 60
Edward, Prince, Earl of Wessex, *68*, 69, 99, 111, 114, *114*, 118, 152, 171, 176
Edwards, Arthur, 121
Egmont, Count of, 74
Eisenhower, Dwight, *126*, *127*
Egypt, 38
Eleanor of Castille, Queen, *53*, 54
Eleanor crosses, 54
Electress Sophia, 83
Electress Sophia Naturalisation Act, 83–84, 85
Elizabeth I, 49, 71, 72, 75, 76, 77, 129
Elizabeth II, *12*, 16, *16*, 17, *17*, 20, 22, 24, 25, *31*, 32, *32*, 36, *37*, 39, 40, 44, 45, 46, 54, 63, 67, 68, 71, 83, *83*, 86, 87, 87, 88, 89, 91, *93*, 94, *95*, 97, *97*, 98, *98*, *101*, 105, 107, *108*, *109*, 117, *117*, 117, *118*, 121, *124*, *127*, *126*; wedding dress, 13–14; wedding gifts, 17–19; wedding ceremony, 19–23; wedding breakfast and honeymoon, 24–26; birth, childhood, education, 31–33; meets Prince Philip, 36; obstacles to marriage, 36, 39; engagement ring, 40; deals with tragedies, 93; Christian faith, 94; on role of Prince Philip, 96; position as Head of Commonwealth, 105; views husband as head of family, 111; and children, 111; and Prince of Wales, 111–112, 119–120; motto as Queen
of Canada, 122; international role of, 123; two natures as Sovereign, 125; Canadian Princess, 127, *140*, *141*, 143, *143*; character, 164; marital relations, 171
Elizabeth the Winter Queen, 48
Elizabeth, Queen Elizabeth the Queen Mother, 16, 17, 21, 26, 31, *31*, *34*, 37, 39, 54, *62*, 63, 94, 100, 102, 107, 111, 115, 116, 117, 120
Empire, British, 44, 45, 80, 82, *82*, 134
Elms School, Saint-Cloud, 30
Erik II, 75
Eton, 120
Eugenie, Princess, of York, 104, 118, *119*
Europe, 127
Everage, "Dame" Edna, 104
Evzones, Greek Royal Guard, *30*
Expo '67, 150
Fagan, Michael, 171
Far East, 38
Falklands War, 120, 132
Fiji, 126
Fine Arts Commission, 81
First Canadian Division, 38
Fitzherbert, Maria, 54, 56
Flag debate, 148
Flanders, 74
Ford, Gerald, 127, *127*
Francis, Dauphin of France, 73
Francis II, 71, *75*, 76, 77
Frederick V, Elector Palatine, 48
Frederika, Queen, 35
French Revolution, 48
Gandhi, Mahatma, 19
Garter, Order of, 41, 60, 79, 80
Gatcombe Park, 117
George I, 84
George II, 48, 51, 54
George III, 45, 49, 51, 54, 56, *59*, 60
George IV, 54, 55, *55*, 57, 59
George V, 18, 29, 30, 31, 32, 34, 45, *46*, 46, 62, 134
George VI, 16, *17*, 26, 31, *31*, 35, 37, 39, 43, 54, *62*, 63, 97, *109*, 111, 131, 132, 134, 143
George I, King of Hellenes, 27, 28, *28*
George, Prince, Duke of Kent, 44, *44*, 48, 63, 67
George Weston Limited, Canada, 40
Gibraltar, 126
Girl Guides, 24, 63
Glamis Castle, 32
Glass Coach, 24
Glorious Revolution, 52–53
Gloucester, Prince William of, 21, 23
Gold State Coach, 104, *124*
Golden Jubilee of Elizabeth II, 32, 100–105, *101*, *103*, *124*, *156*, *160*, 161
Gordonstoun School, 30, 35, 119–120
Government House, Edmonton, 114
Great Depression, 44
Great Exhibition of 1851, 81, *81*
Great Lakes, 132, 134
Greenwich, Baron SEE Philip, Duke of Edinburgh
Grenadier Guards, 24
Greece, 41, 44, 83
Greek Army, 28
Greek Chamber of deputies, 28
Greek coup, 108
Greek Nautical College, 35
Greek Plebiscite on Monarchy, 35
Grenada, 123
Grenadines, 123
Grey, Lady Jane, 74
Guildhall, Bath, 102
Haakon VII, 13, 62
Habsburg, 74
Hanover, Prince Ernest of, 83–84
Hahn, Kurt, 30, 35
Harewood, Earl of, 62, *62*
Harper, Stephen, 139, 140, *140*, 159, 160
Hartnell, Sir Norman, 16
Harry (Henry), Prince, of Wales, 103, 113, 115, 116, *116*, 117, 118, 119, 120, *121*
Head of State, a republican term, 125
Heath, Edward, 102
Henrietta Maria, Queen, 52, *53*
Henry I, 47
Henry II, 76
Henry IV, 78
Henry VII, 78
Henry VIII, 47, 49, 72, 73, 74, 76
Henry, Prince, Duke of Gloucester, 45, *45*
Hesse, Grand Duchy of, 44
Hesse, Grand Duke of, 60
Hesse, Princess Mary, Landgravine of, 48
Hill House School, 119
Holland, 37
Holy Land, 54
Hope, Bob, 98
Horse Guards, 21
Horton, Lady Anne, 54
Hospital For Sick Children, Great Ormond Street, *96*
House of Commons, 49
House of Lords, 56
Household Cavalry, 19
Hovingham Hall, 63
Hyderabad, Nizam of, 19
Imperial College, London, 81
Imperial Conference, 33
Imperial Russian Navy, 62
Indian Ocean, 38
Ionian Islands, 27
Iraq, 120
Ireland, 35, 74
Irish State Coach, 21
Islamic extremists, 130
Jamaica, 104, 123, 126
James I, 48, 49, 51, *53*, 77
James II, 52, *53*, 77, 78
James Francis Edward, Prince of Wales, 52
Jamestown, 90, *92*, 126
Japan, 103, 104
Jean, Michaëlle, 158, 159
Jersey, Lady, 54, 55
Jerusalem, 74
John Paul II, Pope, 94
Johnson, Lyndon, 127
Jones, Tom, 104
Jordan, Mrs., 57

Jordan River, 31, 32
Juan Carlos I, 54
Juliana, Queen, 14
Katherine of Aragon, Queen, 47
Kennedy, John, 127
Kenya, 19, 126
Kensington Palace, 19, 30, 116
Kent, Prince Edward, Duke of, 57, 58
Kent, Prince Edward, Duke of, 63, 103
Kent, Duchess of (Katherine Worsley), 63, *64*
Kent, Princess Victoria, Duchess of, 58
Kent, Prince Michael of, 21, 23
Kentucky, 105
Kentucky Derby, 105
King Consort, 80
King's Dirk, 35
King's Lynn, Norfolk, 102
Kiri Te Kanawa, Dame, 103
Lakefield College, 131, *131*, 152
La Porte, Cadet Matthew, 90
Lascelles, Viscount SEE Harewood, Earl of
Latin America, 127
Laurence, Captain Timothy, 114
Lawrence, Sister Mary, *95*
LeBlanc, Romeo, 159
Leger, Jules, 158
Leibovitz, Anne, 118
Leopold, Prince, of Coburg (King of the Belgians), 56–58, *57*
Libya, 126, 132
Life Guards, 21
Lind, Jenny, 60
London, 26, 31, 33, 52, 54, 131
Lorne, Marquess of (Duke of Argyll), 60
Louise, Princess, Duchess of Argyll, 43
Lynden Manor, Maidenhead, 30
MacDonald, Margaret "Bobo", 16
Major, John, 102
Malcolm III Canmore, 47
Malmesbury, Sir James Harris, Earl of, 54–55
Malta, 111, 126
Mandela, Nelson, 105
Manley, John, 161
Manitoba, 152
Margarita, Princess (Princess Gottfried of Hohenlohe-Langenburg), 108
Marie, Empress of Russia (Dagmar), 27
Marina, Princess, Duchess of Kent, 44, *44*, *44*, 63
Margaret, Queen, 75
Margaret, Princess (Countess of Snowdon), 17, 19, 21, 34, 36, 39, 63, *63*, 67, 100, 117, *117*
Margaret, Princess, 75
Marschner, Joanna, 67
Martin, Paul, 157
Mary I, 47, 71, 72, *72*, 73–75, *73*, 76
Mary II, 48, 49, *54*, 71, 77, *77*, 78, *78*, 79
Mary, Queen, *17*, 18, 19, 21, 30, 31, 33, 45, *45*, *46*, 62, *69*
Mary, Princess Royal (Countess of Harewood), 62, *62*
Mary Adelaide of Cambridge, Princess, 45
Mary of Modena, Queen, 52
Mary Queen of Scots, 71, 72, 75, *75*, 76, *76*, *76*, 77, 85
Matapan, Battle of, 24

Matilda (Edith), Queen, 47
May, Brian, 104
McAdam, W.A., Agent-General of British Columbia, *19*
McCartney, Sir Paul, 104
Mediterranean, 38, 131, 134
Melbourne, Lord, 56, 80
Merioneth, Earl of SEE Philip, Duke of Edinburgh, 41
Mey, Castle of, 102
Michael, King, 13, 54
Milford Haven (Prince Louis of Battenberg), 1st Marquess of, 28, 29; George, 2nd Marquess of, 30; David, 3rd Marquess of, 19, 21, 38–39
Middleton, Kate, 120–121
Milford Haven (Princess Victoria of Hesse), Marchioness of, 28, 30
Milan, 74
Miller, Rt Revd John, 102
Mint Advisory Committee, 98
Mirren, Dame Helen, 115
Modena, 52
Monaco, 30
Monastery of Las Huelgas, Burgos, 54
Mon Repos, 27, *29*
Monsieur Henri, 17
Morocco, 128
Morton, Andrew, 113
Mountbatten, Earl Mountbatten of Burma (Lord Louis), 17, 29, 35, 36, 85, 166
Mountbatten, Countess Mountbatten of Burma (Lady Patricia), 9, 11, 20, 97, 115, 116, 117, 118, 120, 121, 171
Mountbatten, Lady Pamela (Lady Pamela Hicks), 17
Mountbatten, adopted as surname by Prince Philip, 83
Mountbatten, House of, 85, 87
Mozambique, 105
Mulroney, Brian, 155, 156
Naples, Kingdom of, 74
National Archives, London, 13
National Playing Fields Association, 97
National Service of Thanksgiving, 104
National War Memorial, Ottawa, 96
Nazis, 30
New Brunswick, 155
Newfoundland, 131
New York, 81, 91
New Zealand, 32, 35, 63, 96, 104, 126, 129, 131, 134
Nicholas II, 44, *50*
Nixon, Richard, 127
Norman dynasty, 47, 85
North Sea, 51, 131
Northern Ireland, 102
Norway, King of, 14
Norway, 37
Nova Scotia, *113*
Nunavut, 157
Nuptial Drawing Room, 48, 49
Oatlands, 57
Occasional Conformity Bill, 79
Ogilvy, Hon. Sir Angus, 65
Olga, Queen, 35
Ontario, 155
Orange, Prince William of, 51

Order of Canada, *149*, 150, 153, 161
Osborne House, 60, 82
Osbourne, Ozzy, 104
Ottawa, 131, 135
Oslo, 51
Otto I, 27
Ottoman Empire, 27
Pacific, 88, 132, 134
Panama, 126
Papua New Guinea, 123
Party at the Palace, 104
Paul I, King of the Hellenes, 35
Pearson, Lester, 148, 150
Pergami, Bartolomeo, 56
Petty Officers' Training School, 39
Philip II, 48, 71, 73–75, *73*, 77
Philip, Duke of Edinburgh, 11, *13*, 14, 17, *18*, 19, 21, 22, *26*, 27, 29, *35*, *38*, 54, 63, *63*, 67, *68*, 71, 79, *83*, *84*, *86*, 87, *87*, 89, *91*, *92*, 93, 97, *97*, *99*, *101*, 104, 107, 108, *108*, *110*, 112, *116*, 121, *124*, 139, *140*, *142*, *143*, 150, 151, *151*, 152, 163; wedding gift to bride, 18; parents, 28–30; childhood, 30; and Greece, 35; meets Princess Elizabeth, 36; war experience, 38; suitability as spouse for Princess, 41; renounces place in succession to Greek Crown, 83; born a British subject under Sophia Naturalisation Act, 83–4; Canadian Prime Minister suggests he be made Prince of the Commonwealth, 85; created Canadian Privy Councillor, 85; longest consort to Queen, 87; influence on Queen, 96; developed royal role for himself, 96–100; Duke of Edinburgh's Award Scheme, 99–100; and upbringing of Prince of Wales, 119–120; can act in three capacities, Queen in only one, 125; character, 164, 166; abandonment of naval career, 167, 168; press rumours, 169, 170; created Prince of the United Kingdom, 170; marital relations, 171
Phillips, Capt. Mark, *66*, 67, 112
Phillips, Peter, 117, *118*
Phillips, Zara, 117, *118*
Picadilly Street, Number 145, 32
Plantagenet dynasty, 85
Poet's Corner, 21
Prince Consort, title of, 80
Prince Edward Island, 152
Prince of the Commonwealth, 85
Privy Council, Most Honourable, 56
Privy Council for Canada, Queen's, 69, *84*, 85, 145, 154
Prom at the Palace, 102, 104
Prophet Mohammed, 128
Prussia, 41
Quebec, 148, 154, 155, *165*
Queen, 104
Queen's Bays Regiment, 67
Queen's Gallery, Buckingham Palace, 32
Queen's House, Kew, 58
Queen's Private Secretary, 80
Rayne, Edward, 17
Reagan, Ronald, 127
Regent Designate, 80, 85
Reifel Island Migratory Bird Sanctuary, *100*

Renard, Simon, 73
Richmond, Virginia, 89, *90*
Rideau Hall, 33, 34, 143, *143*, 152, 158, 159
Romania, Queen Mother of (Helen), 13
Romanovs, 27
Roosevelt, Franklin, 134
Rostropovich, Mstislav, 103
Royal Ascot, 113
Royal Canadian Mint, *105*
Royal Canadian Mounted Police (RCMP), 124, 139
Royal Collection, 32, 81
Royal Hellenic Navy, 35
Royal Lodge, Windsor Great Park, 32, 109
Royal London Hospital, 95
Royal marriage ritual, 49
Royal Marriages Act, 54
Royal Marriages Bill, 74
Royal Marriage Stakes, *58*
Royal Naval College, Dartmouth, 35, 36
Royal Navy, 35, 37, 38, 83
Royal walkabout, 96
Royal Wedding Dresses, The, 67
Royal weddings, 43, 48–49; post-Georgian period, 59–60; Victorian, 60–62; post–World War I, 62–63; reign of Elizabeth II, 63–70; current practices, 69; important, popular state affairs, 70
Royal wedding souvenirs, 13
Russia, 41, 112
Russian tiara, 17
Saint-Cloud, 30
St. Andrew's University, 120
St. Anne's Cathedral, Belfast, 102
Saint Christopher and Nevis, 123
St. George's Chapel, Windsor, 60, *68*, 103, 114
St. James's Palace, 48, 49
St. Laurent, Louis, 144, 158
St Lawrence Seaway, 126, 132, 147
Saint Lucia, 123
St. Margaret, 47
St. Mildred, Church of, 61
St. Paul's Cathedral, 67, 104
St. Thomas, Church of, 91
Saint Vincent, 123
Salem School, Baden, 30
Salic law, 72
Salisbury, Frank, 62
Sarah, Duchess of York (Sarah Ferguson), *68*, 112, 113, *113*, 114
Saskatchewan, 155, 161
Saudi Arabia, 125
Sauvé, Jean, 159
Saxe-Coburg-Gotha, Ernst, Duke of, 80
Saxe-Coburg-Gotha, Prince Ernest of, 54
Saxe-Coburg-Gotha, House of, 85
Scandinavia, 51
Schloss Ehrenburg, 58
Scotland, 51, 131
Shakespeare, William, 72

Shawcross, William, 118
Sheen Lodge, 47
Sicily, 38, 74
Silver Jubilee, 152, 153
Smyrna, Battle of, 28
Snowdon, Anthony Armstrong-Jones, Earl of, 63, *63*, 93, 117
Solomon Islands, 123
Sophie, Queen of the Hellenes, 35
Sophie, Princess (Princess Christopher of Hesse), 108
Sophie, Countess of Wessex (Sophie Rhys-Jones), *68*, 69, 114, *114*, 118, 121
South Africa, 35, 39, 105, 134
South Atlantic, 132
Spain, Royal Family of, 14
Spanish Armada, 72, 74, 75
Special Entry Cadet, 35
Spencer, Earl, 116, *116*
Sports Personality of the Year Award, 118
State Opening of Parliament, 129
Statute of Westminster, 33, 134, 145
Strathmore and Kinghorne, Earl of, 31
Strathmore and Kinghorne, Countess of, 31
Stuart dynasty, 85
Susan, Elizabeth II's favourite corgi, 26
Susan Constant, 92
Switzerland, 30
Tang Dynasty, 128
Television, 134, 135, 137
Test Act, 79
Thames, 52
Thatcher, Margaret, 102
Theodora, Princess (Margravine Berthold of Baden), 108
The Queen, 115
Thomas, J.H., 34
Timbertops School, 131
Tomb of the Unknown Warrior, 23
Tonga, 126
Tonga, Queen Salote of, 14
Townsend, Group Captain Peter, 117
Treetops Hotel, 97, *98*
Trudeau, Pierre, 153, 154
Truman, Harry, 19, *126*, 127
Tudor dynasty, 85
Tuvalu, 123
Tyrol, 74
Uganda, 126
United Kingdom, 130, 142
United States, 37, 80, 82, 89, *91*, 110, 125, 126, 127, 131, 134
Valiant, HMS, 24, 38, 142
Vanity Fair, 118
VE Day, 39
Victoria Cross, 156
Victoria, Queen, 27, 28, 41, 47, 48, *50*, 54, 58, *59*, 60, 61, *61*, 69, *69*, 79–80, 82–83, *80*, *81*, *82*, 85, 97, 104, 131

Victoria, Princess Royal, 69,
Victoria and Albert, HMY (I, II & III), 36, 131, 132
Victoria Memorial, 103
Vimy, 139, 140, *141*, *142*, 159
Virgin Queen, 75
Virginia, 90, *91*, 105
Wales, Prince of SEE Charles
Wales, Prince of SEE Edward VII
Wales, Prince of SEE George IV
Wales, Prince of SEE George V
Wales, Prince of SEE James Francis Edward
Wales, Prince of SEE Windsor, Duke of
Wales, Princess of SEE Alexandra, Queen
Wales, Princess Charlotte of, 56–58, *58*, 59
Wales, Princess of SEE Diana
Wales, Princess Maud of (Queen of Norway), 62
Wallace, HMS, 38
Wars of the Roses, 72
Waterloo Gallery, Windsor Castle, 62
Waterloo Station, 26
Wedding anniversaries, 19, *164*, 170, *170*, *176*
Wells, H.G., 29
Welsh gold, 23, 69
Westminster Abbey, 14, 19, 21, 23, 24, 43, 44, 47, 63, 67, *68*
Westminster, Dean of, 23, 48
Westmoreland, Earl of, 79
Whig nobles, 52
Whitechapel Royal Hospital, 95
Whitehall Palace, 52
Wick, 102
William, Prince, of Wales, 103, 107, 113, 115, 117, *118*, 119, 120, *121*
William III, 48, 49, 52, *54*, 71, 77, *77*, 78, *78*, 79, *80*
William IV (Duke of Clarence), 56, 57, 58
William the Conqueror, 78
Williamsburg, Virginia, *91*
Williamson, John T., 19
Winchester Cathedral, 48
Windsor Castle, 24, 33, 37, 38, 62, *82*, 94–95, 114, 115
Windsor, Duke of (Edward VIII), 14, 34, *34*, 49, 134, 139, *141*, 163
Windsor, Duchess of (Wallis Simpson), 14, 34
Windsor, House of, 85, 87
Windsor, Lady Louise, 118
Windsor-Mountbatten, House of, 85
Winter Palace, St. Petersburg, 48
Wireless, 134
World Trade Center, 91
World Wide Fund For Nature (WWF), 98, *100*
Wyatt, Sir Thomas, 74
York, Prince Frederick, Duke of, 48, 49, 57
York Princess Frederica, Duchess of York, 48
Yugoslavia, King of, 13
Yugoslavia, Queen of, 13